Music transcriptions by Pete Billmann, Jeff Jacobson and David Stocker

ISBN 0-634-07880-1

7777 W. BLUEMOUND RD. P.O. BOX 13819 MILWAUKEE, WI 53213

In Australia Contact:
Hal Leonard Australia Pty. Ltd.
22 Taunton Drive P.O. Box 5130
Cheltenham East, 3192 Victoria, Australia
Email: ausadmin@halleonard.com

Visit Hal Leonard Online at
www.halleonard.com

Megalomaniac

Words and Music by Brandon Boyd, Michael Einziger, Jose Pasillas II, Chris Kilmore and Ben Kenney

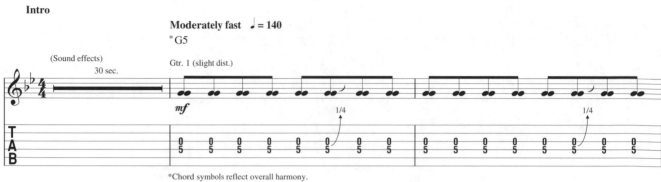

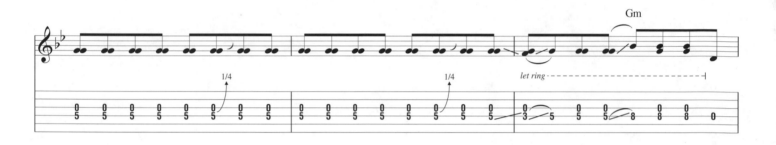

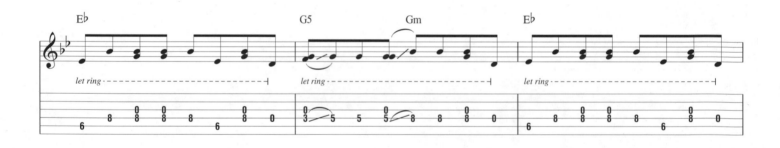

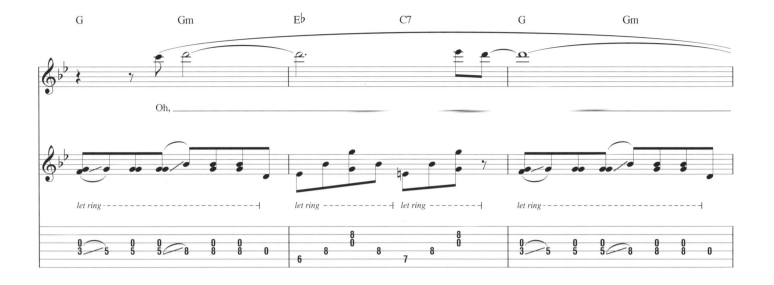

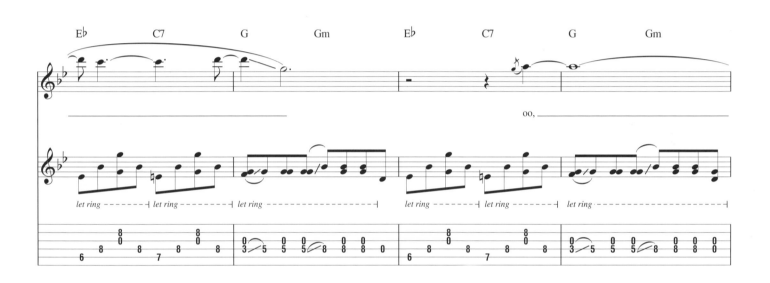

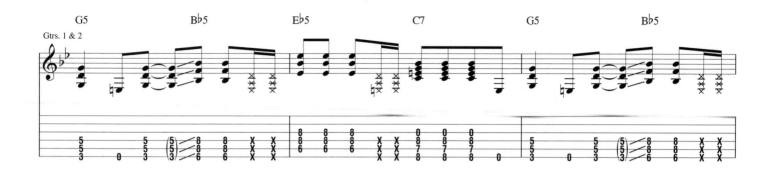

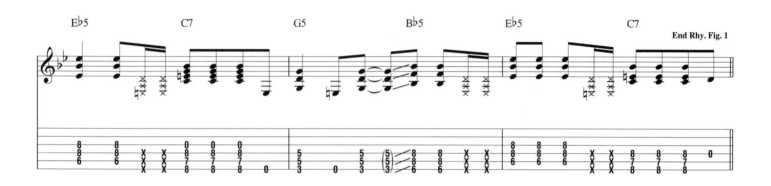

Verse

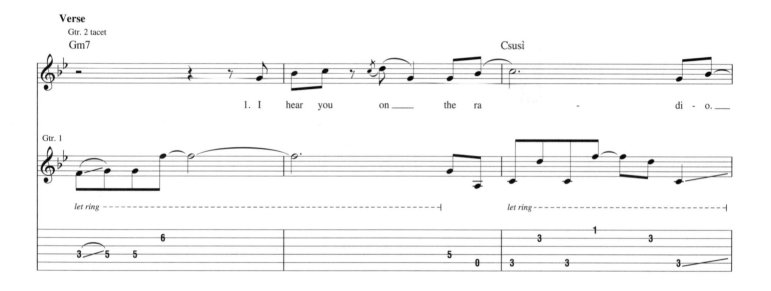

1. I hear you on ____ the ra - di - o. ____

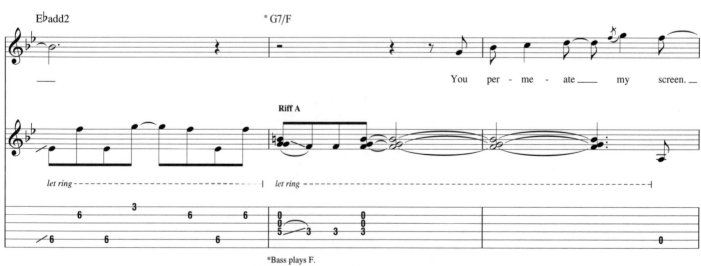

____ You per - me - ate ____ my screen. ___

*Bass plays F.

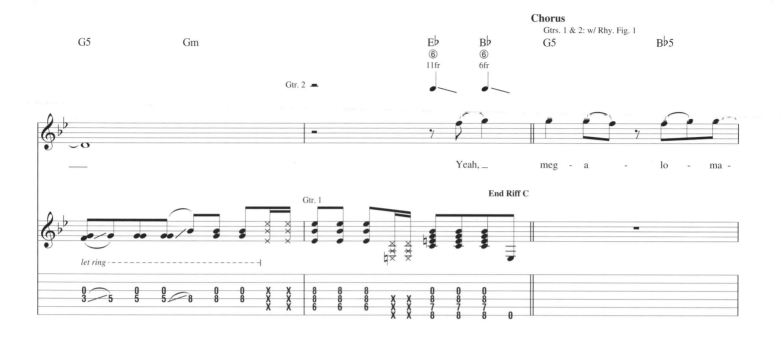

Chorus

Gtrs. 1 & 2: w/ Rhy. Fig. 1

G5　　　Gm　　　Eb　Bb　G5　　　Bb5

Yeah,___ meg - a - lo - ma -

End Riff C

Gtr. 1

let ring

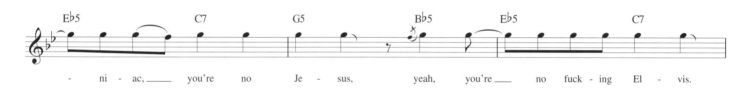

Eb5　　　C7　　　G5　　　Bb5　　　Eb5　　　C7

- ni - ac,_____ you're no Je - sus, yeah, you're___ no fuck - ing El - vis.

G5　　　Bb5　　　Eb5　　　C7　　　G5　　　Bb5　　　Eb5　　　C7

Wash your___ hands clean of _____ your - self, ba - by, and step down,___ step down,___ step down.

Interlude

Gm7　　　　　　　　　　　Ebadd2　　　　　　Csus²

Oo. _____

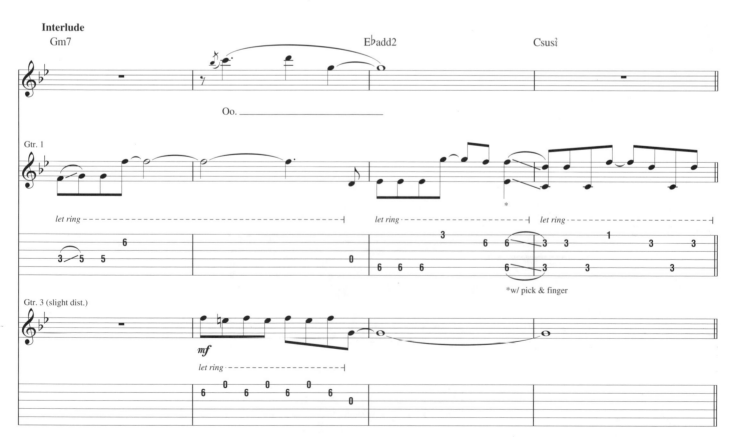

Gtr. 1

let ring

*w/ pick & finger

Gtr. 3 (slight dist.)

mf

let ring

Verse

Gtr. 1: w/ Riff B
Gtr. 3 tacet

2. If I were your ap - pend - ag - es

Gtr. 1: w/ Riff A

I'd hold o - pen your eyes so you would see

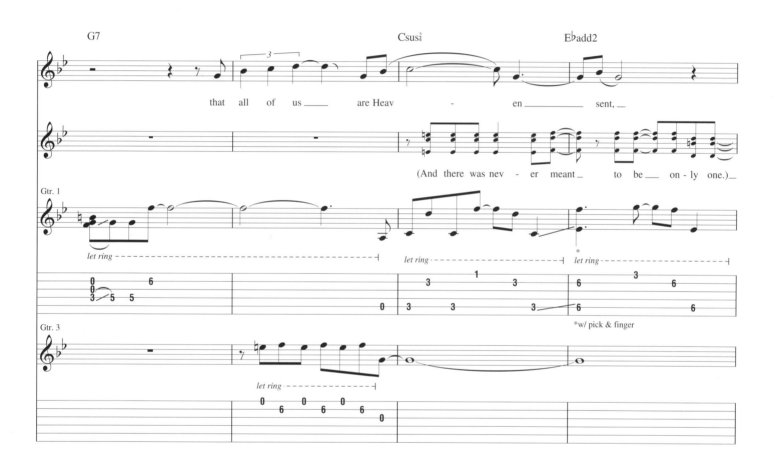

that all of us are Heav - en sent,

(And there was nev - er meant to be on - ly one.)

*w/ pick & finger

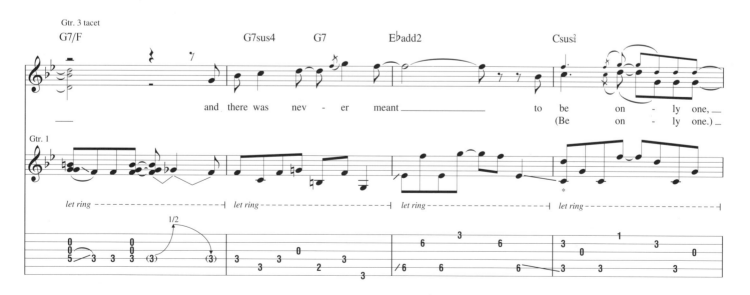

and there was nev - er meant to be on - ly one,
(Be on - ly one.)

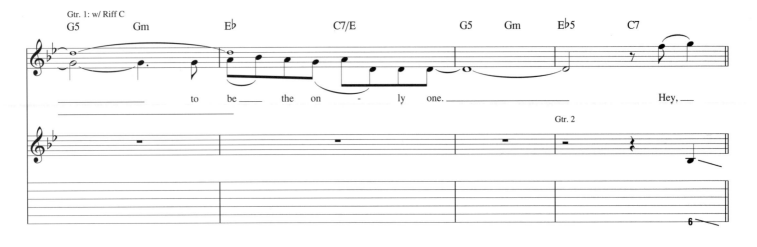

to be____ the on - ly one._____ Hey,____

𝄋 Chorus

Gtrs. 1 & 2: w/ Rhy. Fig. 1 (2 times)
2nd time, Gtrs. 1 & 2: w/ Rhy. Fig. 1 (1 7/8 times)

meg - a - lo - ma - ni - ac,____ you're no Je - sus, yeah, you're__ no fuck - ing El - vis.

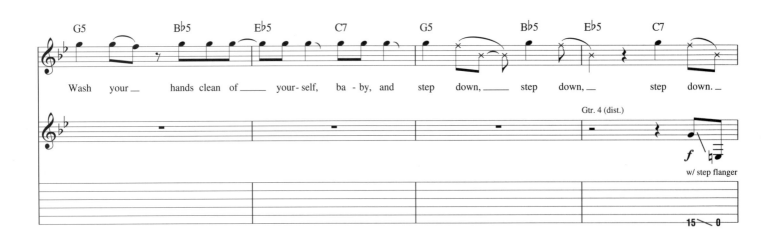

Wash your__ hands clean of____ your-self, ba - by, and step down,____ step down,__ step down.__

Gtr. 4 (dist.)

w/ step flanger

Gtr. 4: w/ Rhy. Fig. 1
2nd time, Gtr. 4: w/ Rhy. Fig. 1 (1st 7 meas.)

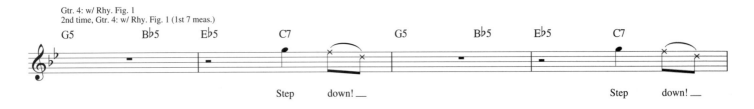

Step down!__ Step down!__

To Coda ⊕   **Interlude**

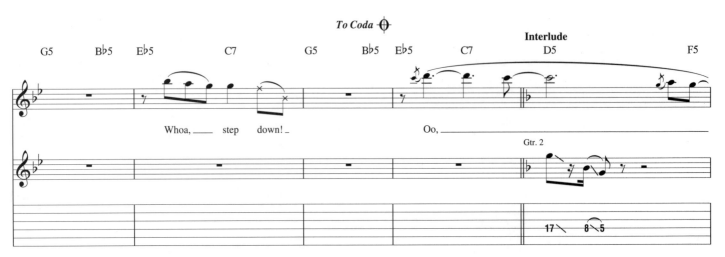

Whoa,__ step down!__ Oo,_____

Gtr. 2

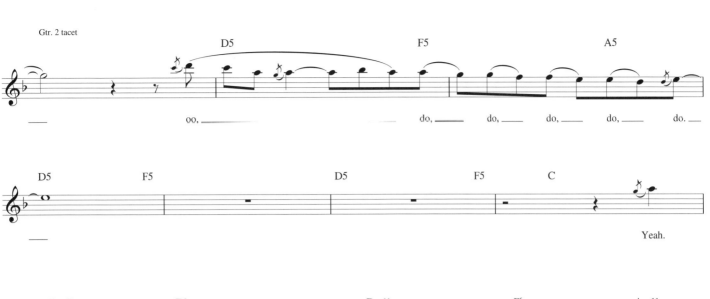

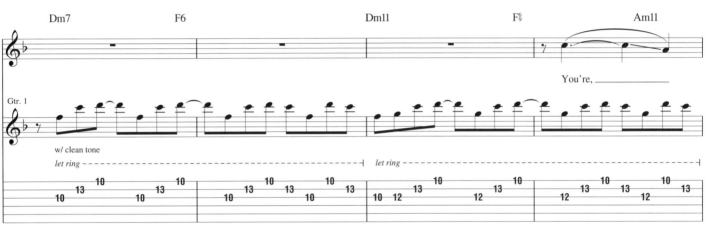

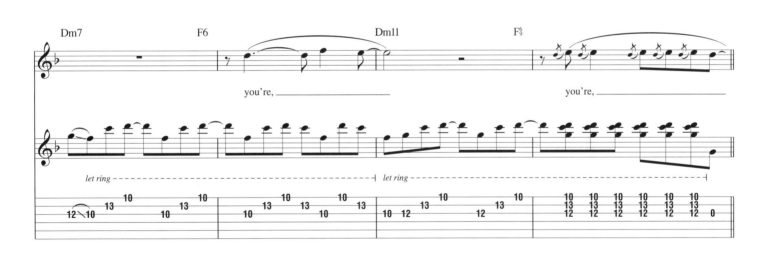

9

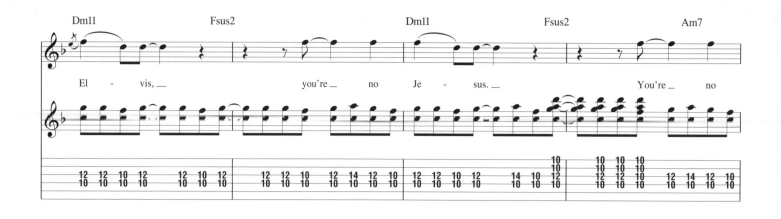

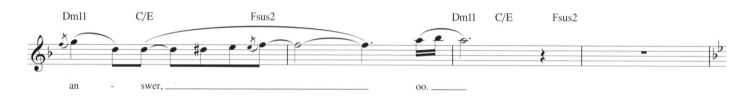

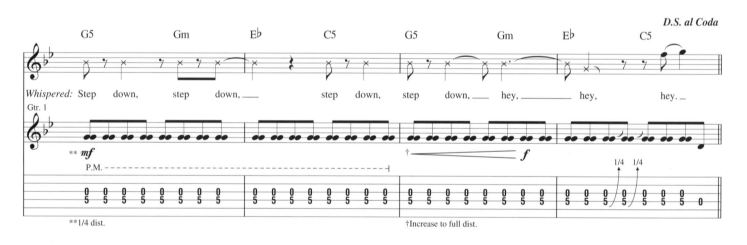

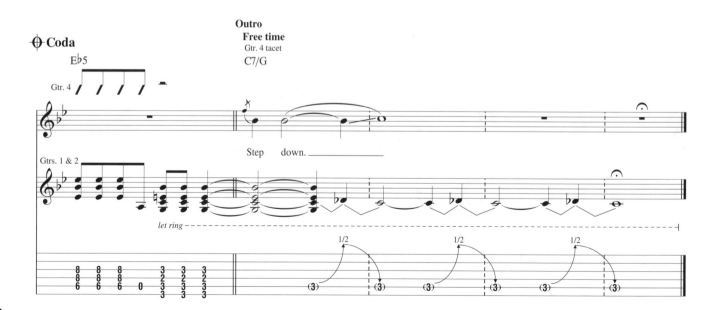

A Crow Left of the Murder

Words and Music by Brandon Boyd, Michael Einziger, Jose Pasillas II, Chris Kilmore and Ben Kenney

*Chord symbols reflect overall harmony.

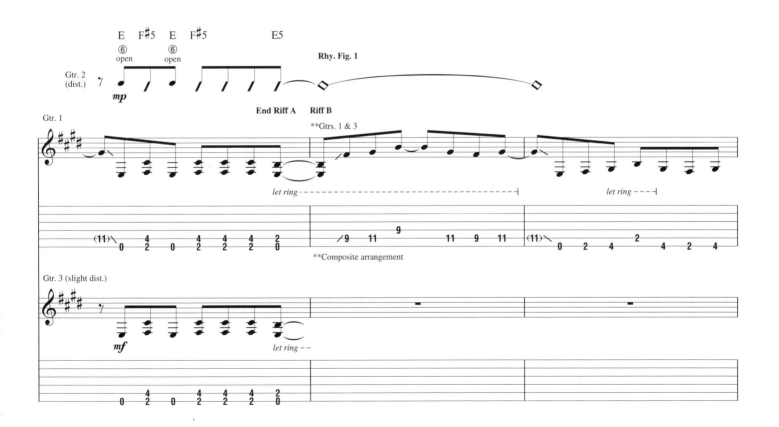

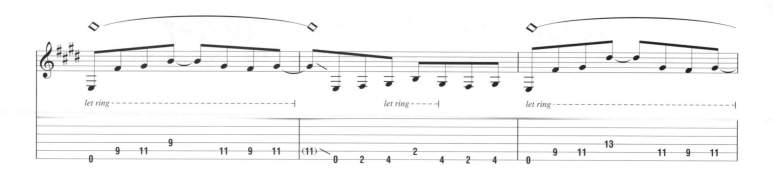

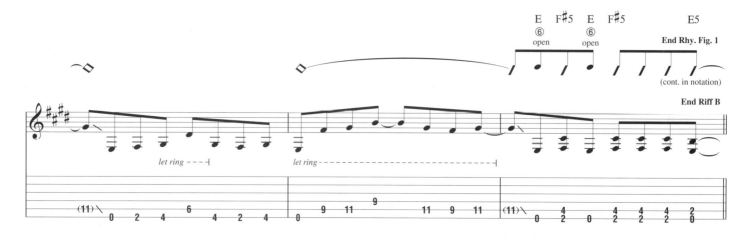

End Rhy. Fig. 1

End Riff B

ॐ Verse

Gtrs. 1 & 3: w/ Riff B (1 7/8 times)
2nd time, Gtrs. 1 & 3: w/ Riff A
Gtr. 2: w/ Rhy. Fig. 1 (1 7/8 times)
2nd time, Gtr. 4: w/ Fill 1

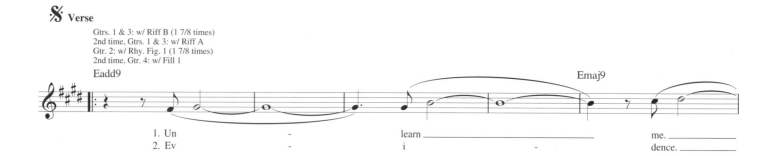

1. Un - learn _____ me. _____
2. Ev - i - dence. _____

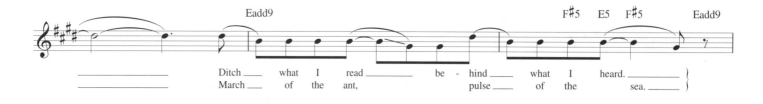

Ditch ____ what I read _____ be - hind ____ what I heard. ____
March ____ of the ant, pulse ____ of the sea. ____

2nd time, Gtrs. 1 & 3: w/ Riff B (1st 7 meas.)

Look, _____ find, _____

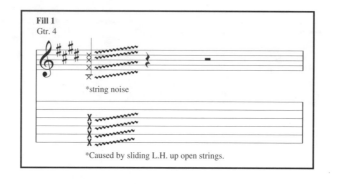

Fill 1
Gtr. 4

*string noise

*Caused by sliding L.H. up open strings.

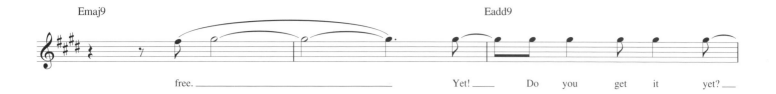

Chorus

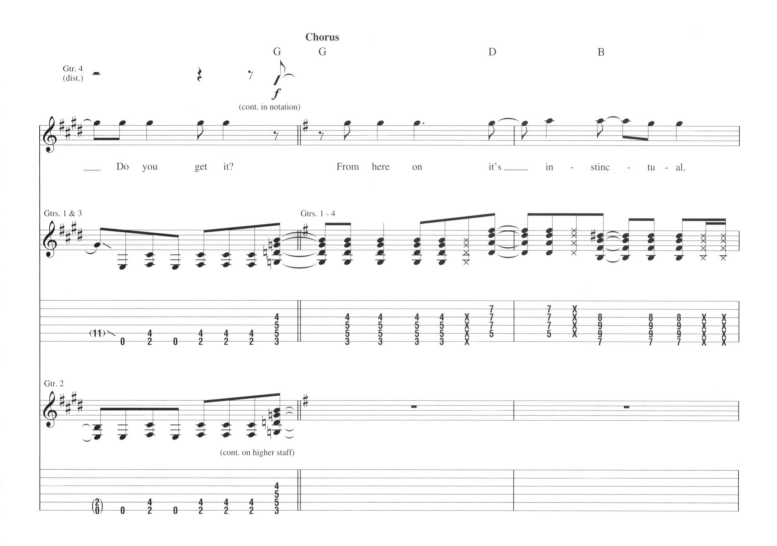

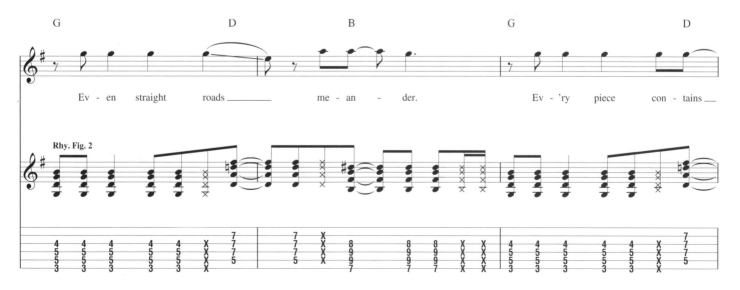

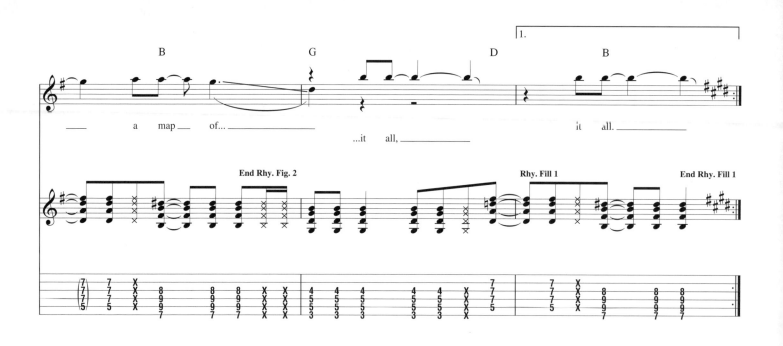

a map ___ of... _____

...it all, _____

it all. _____

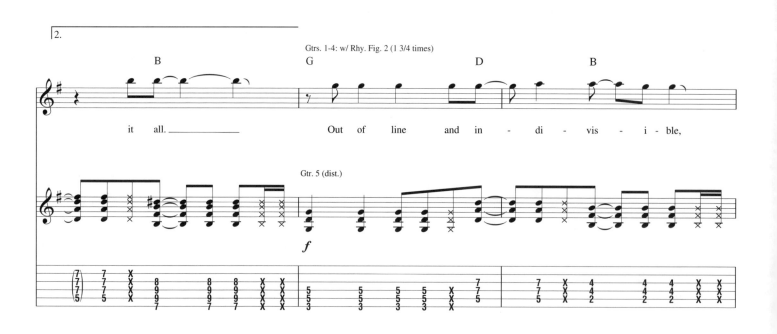

it all. _____

Out of line and in - di - vis - i - ble,

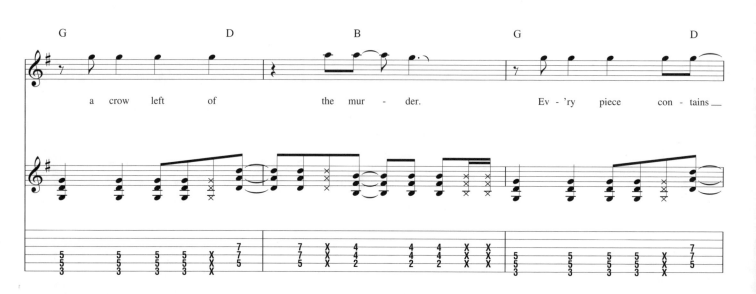

a crow left of the mur - der. Ev - 'ry piece con - tains ___

15

Bridge

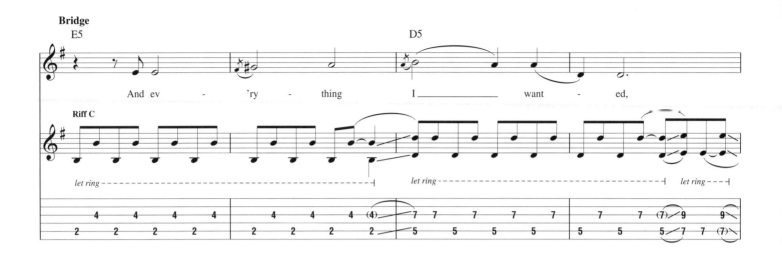

And ev - 'ry - thing I _____ want - ed,

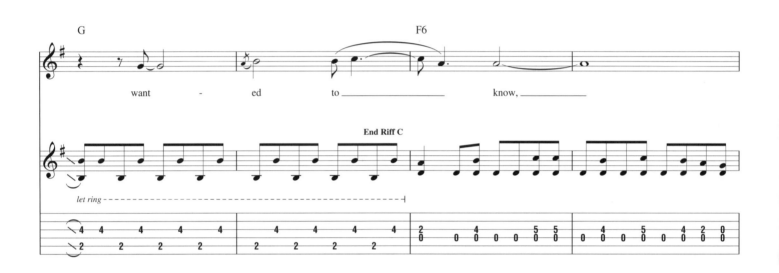

want - ed to _____ know, _____

Gtr. 1: w/ Riff C

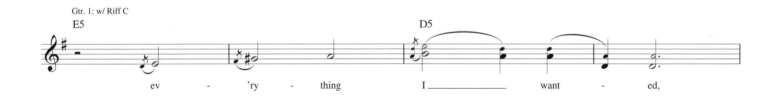

ev - 'ry - thing I _____ want - ed,

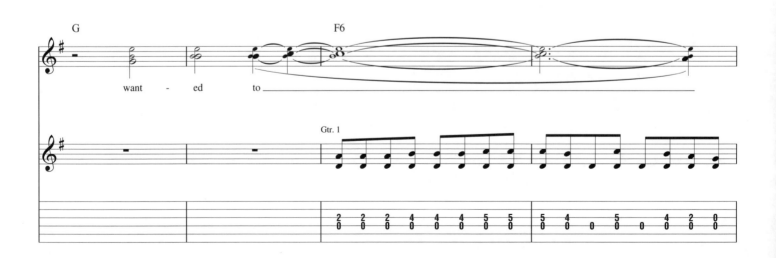

want - ed to _____

Half-time feel

Gtr. 1 tacet

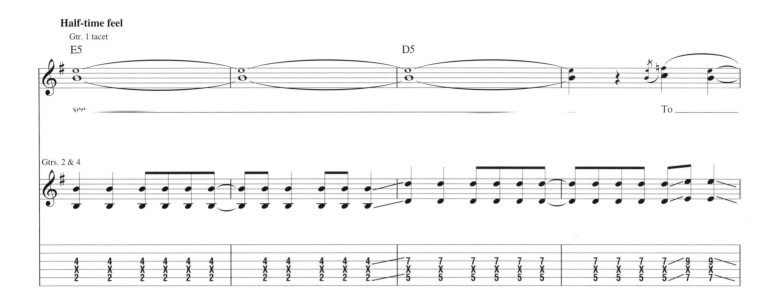

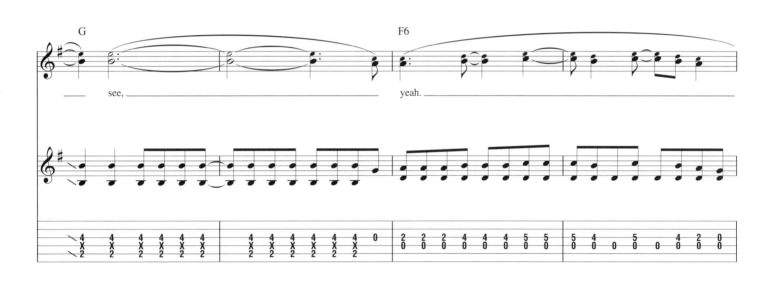

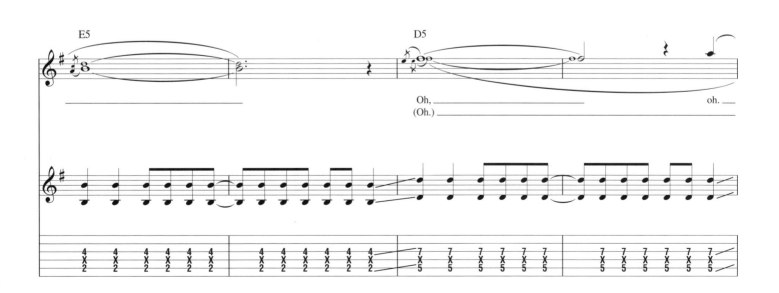

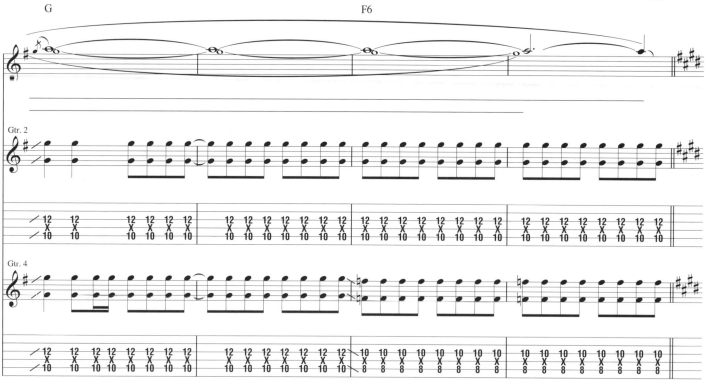

Verse

*Gtr. 1: w/ Riff A
Gtrs. 2 & 4 tacet

*w/ slight dist.

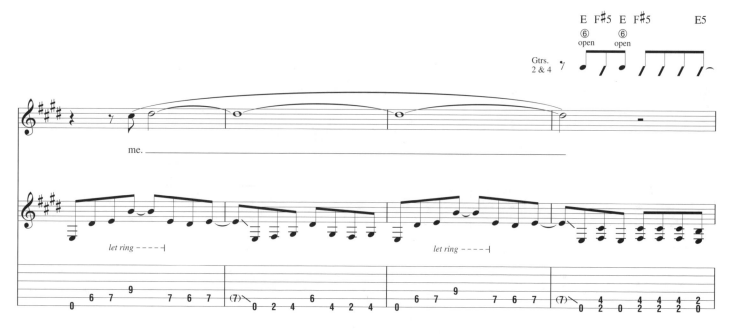

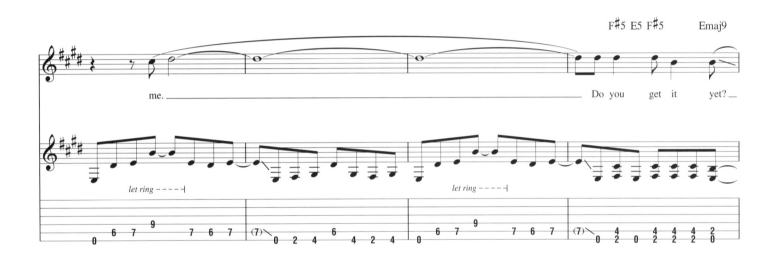

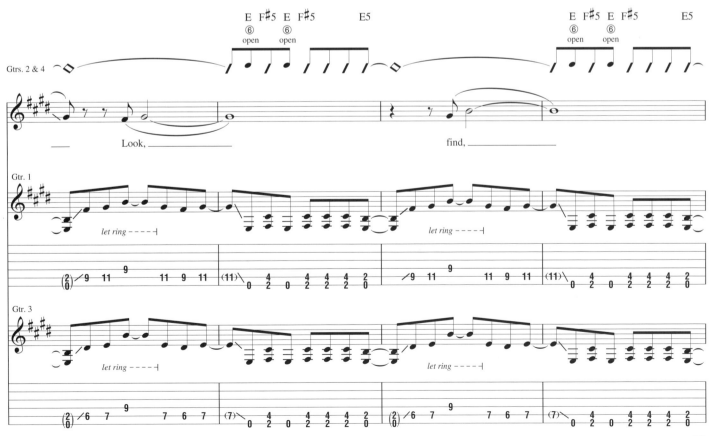

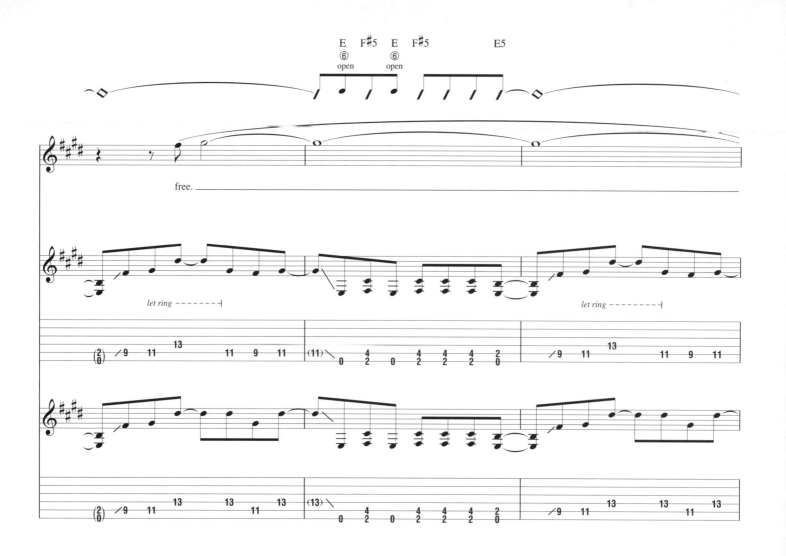

Outro

Gtrs. 2 & 4 tacet

Do you get it yet?___ Do you get it yet?___

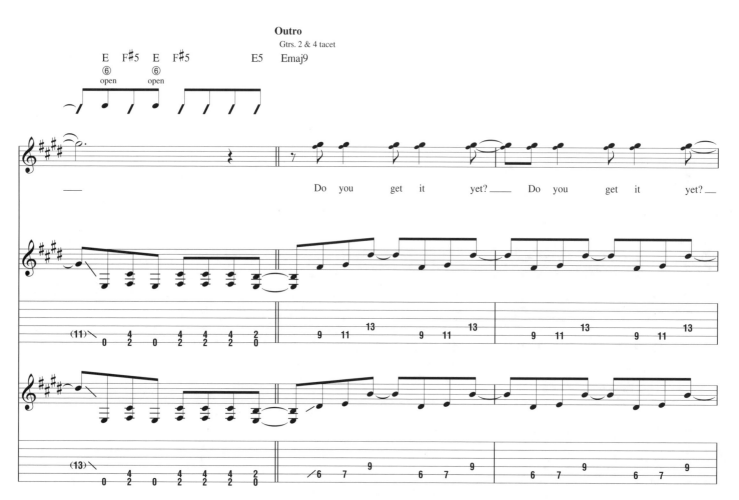

Do you get it yet? Do you get it yet? Do you get it yet?

Fade out

E F#5 E F#5 E5

Do you get it yet? Do you get it yet?

Agoraphobia

Words and Music by Brandon Boyd, Michael Einziger, Jose Pasillas II, Chris Kilmore and Ben Kenney

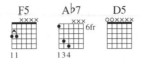

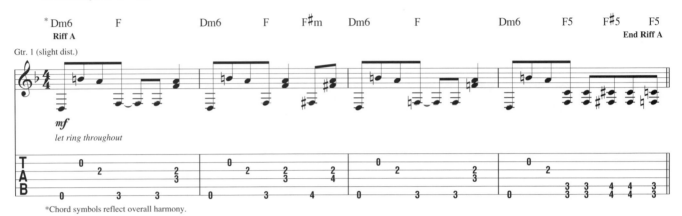

Drop D tuning:
(low to high) D-A-D-G-B-E

Intro
Moderately fast ♩ = 122

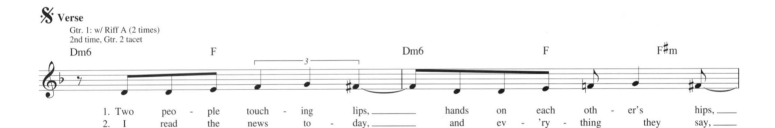

*Chord symbols reflect overall harmony.

Verse

Gtr. 1: w/ Riff A (2 times)
2nd time, Gtr. 2 tacet

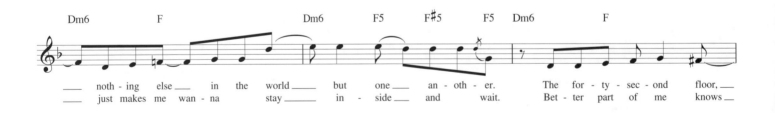

1. Two peo-ple touch-ing lips, _____ hands on each oth-er's hips, _____
2. I read the news to-day, _____ and ev-'ry-thing they say, _____

_____ noth-ing else in the world _____ but one an-oth-er. The for-ty-sec-ond floor, _____
_____ just makes me wan-na stay _____ in-side _____ and wait. Bet-ter part of me knows _____

_____ on a dis-tant shore, _____ I won-der how we've strayed _____ so far _____ from this.
_____ that wait-ing in the throws _____ is on a par with read-ing with my eyes closed.

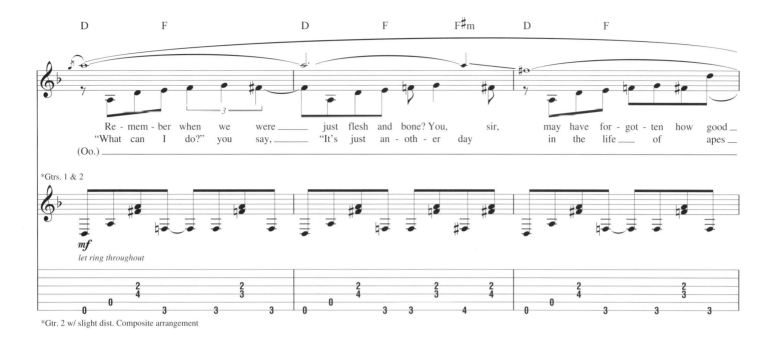

*Gtrs. 1 & 2

*Gtr. 2 w/ slight dist. Composite arrangement

Pre-Chorus
Half-time feel
Gtr. 2 tacet

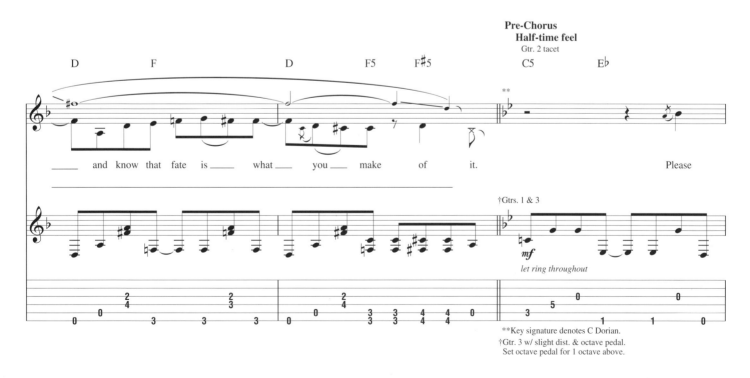

**Key signature denotes C Dorian.
†Gtr. 3 w/ slight dist. & octave pedal.
Set octave pedal for 1 octave above.

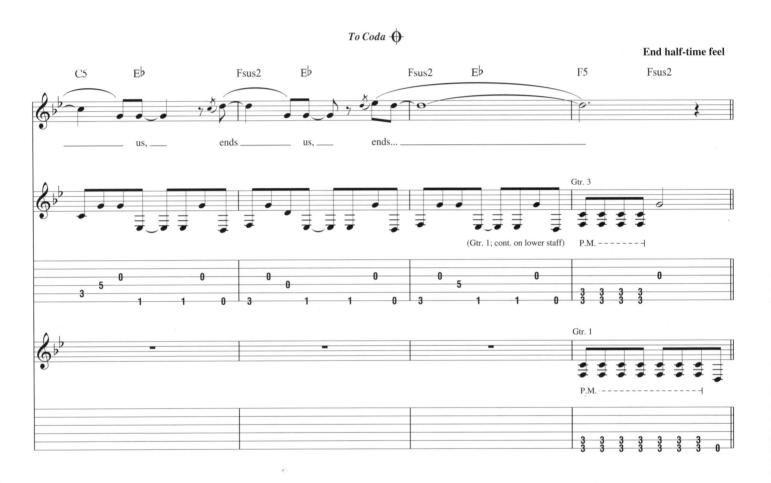

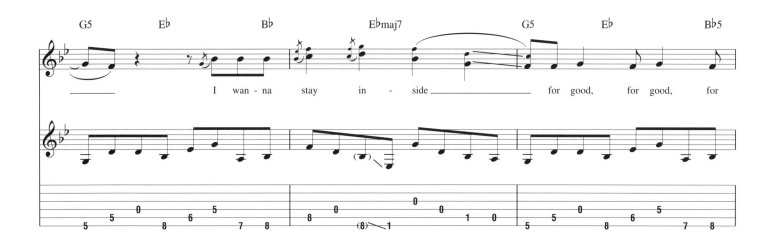

I wan-na stay in-side _____ for good, for good, for

D.S. al Coda

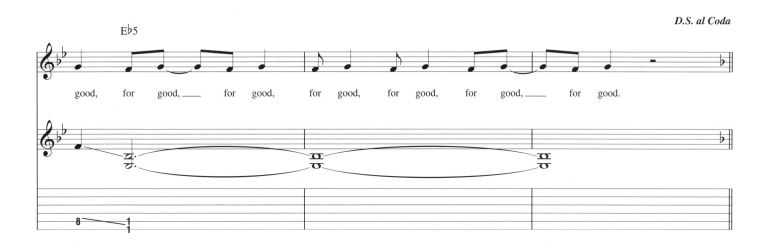

good, for good, ____ for good, for good, for good, for good, ____ for good.

End half-time feel

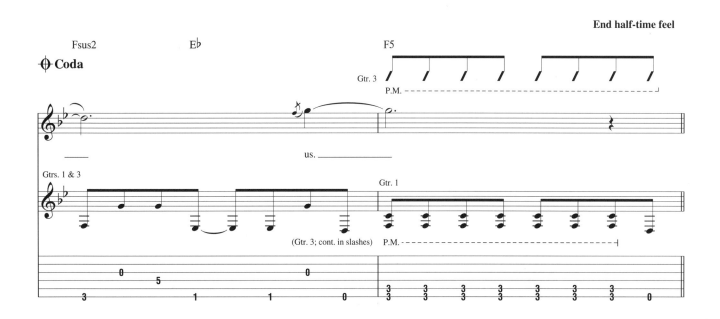

Coda

us. _____

Chorus

Gtrs. 1 & 2: w/ Riff B (1 3/4 times)
Gtr. 3 tacet

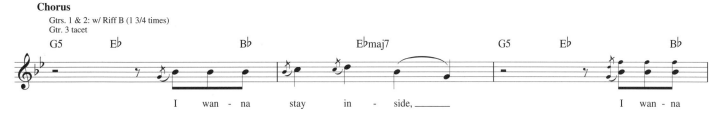

I wan-na stay in-side, _____ I wan-na

25

stay _____ in - side for good. _____

Interlude
Half-time feel

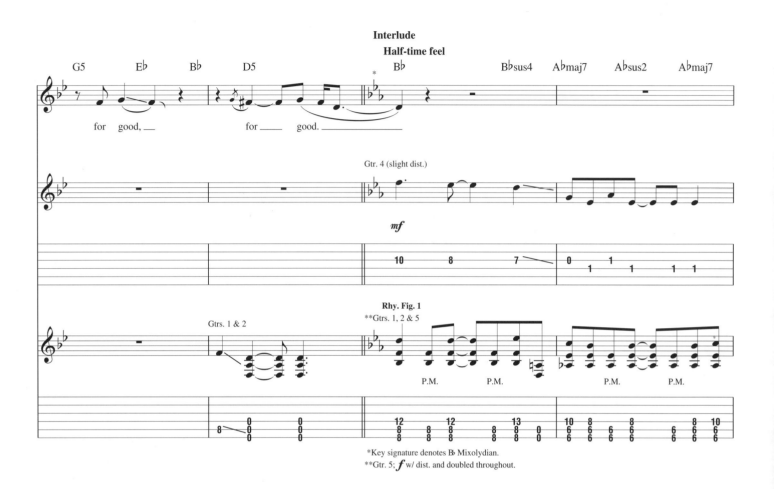

for good, _____ for _____ good. _____

Gtr. 4 (slight dist.)

mf

Rhy. Fig. 1
Gtrs. 1, 2 & 5

Gtrs. 1 & 2

P.M.   P.M.   P.M.   P.M.

*Key signature denotes B♭ Mixolydian.
**Gtr. 5; *f* w/ dist. and doubled throughout.

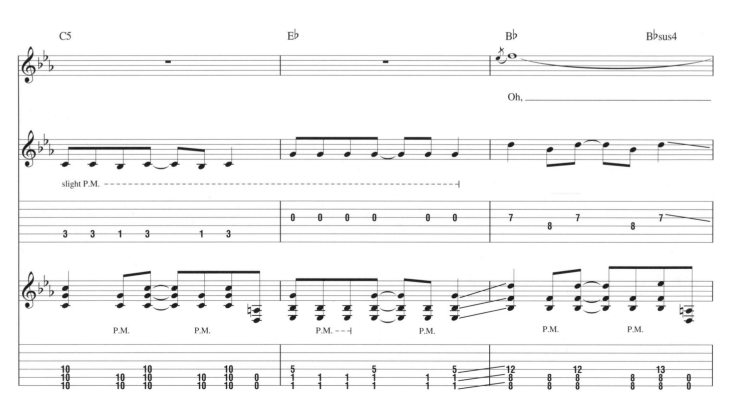

Oh, _____

slight P.M. ---

P.M.   P.M.   P.M. - -   P.M.   P.M.   P.M.

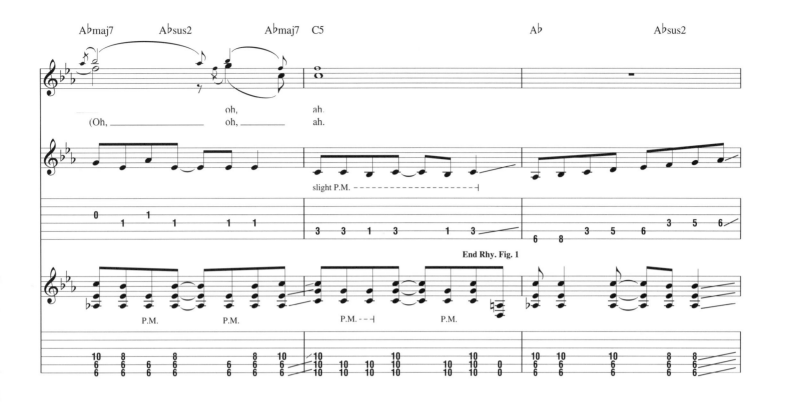

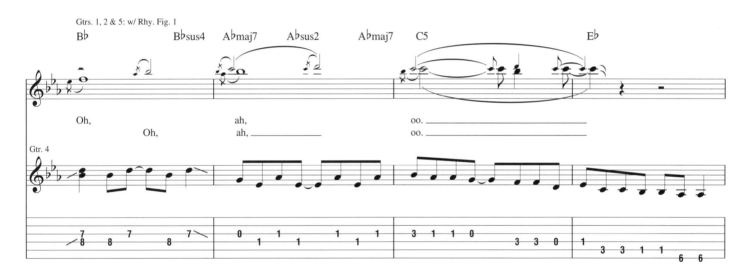

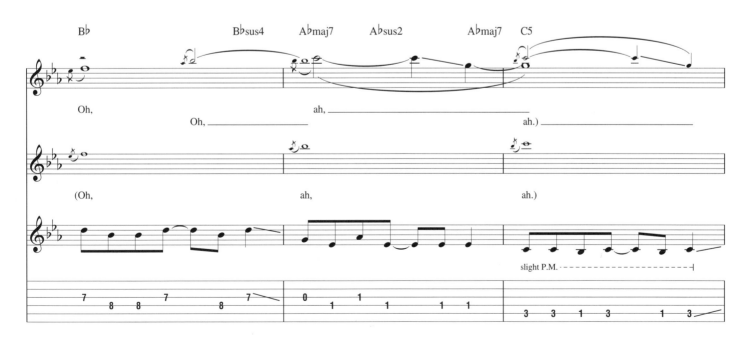

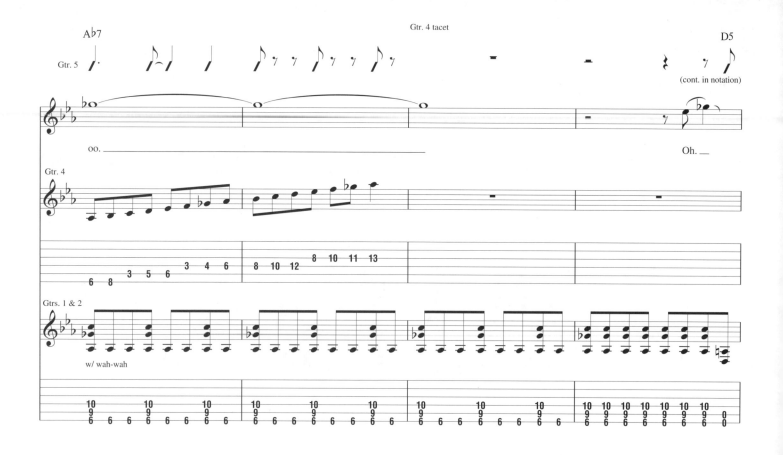

Outro-Chorus

I'm gon-na stay in - side, ___ I'm gon-na stay ___ in - side for good. ___

*Vocs. gradually fade out.

Talk Shows on Mute

Words and Music by Brandon Boyd, Michael Einziger, Jose Pasillas II, Chris Kilmore and Ben Kenney

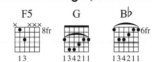

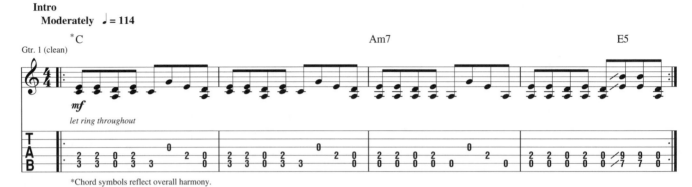

*Chord symbols reflect overall harmony.

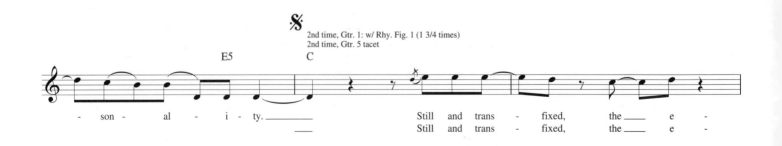

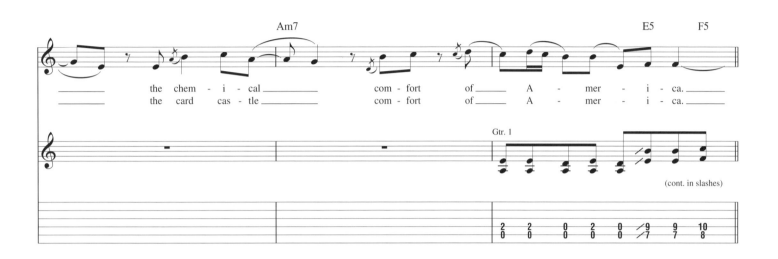

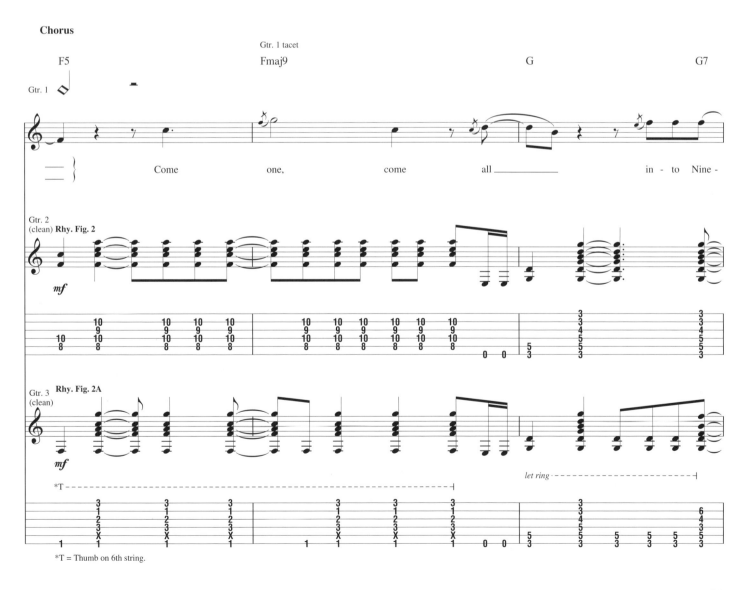

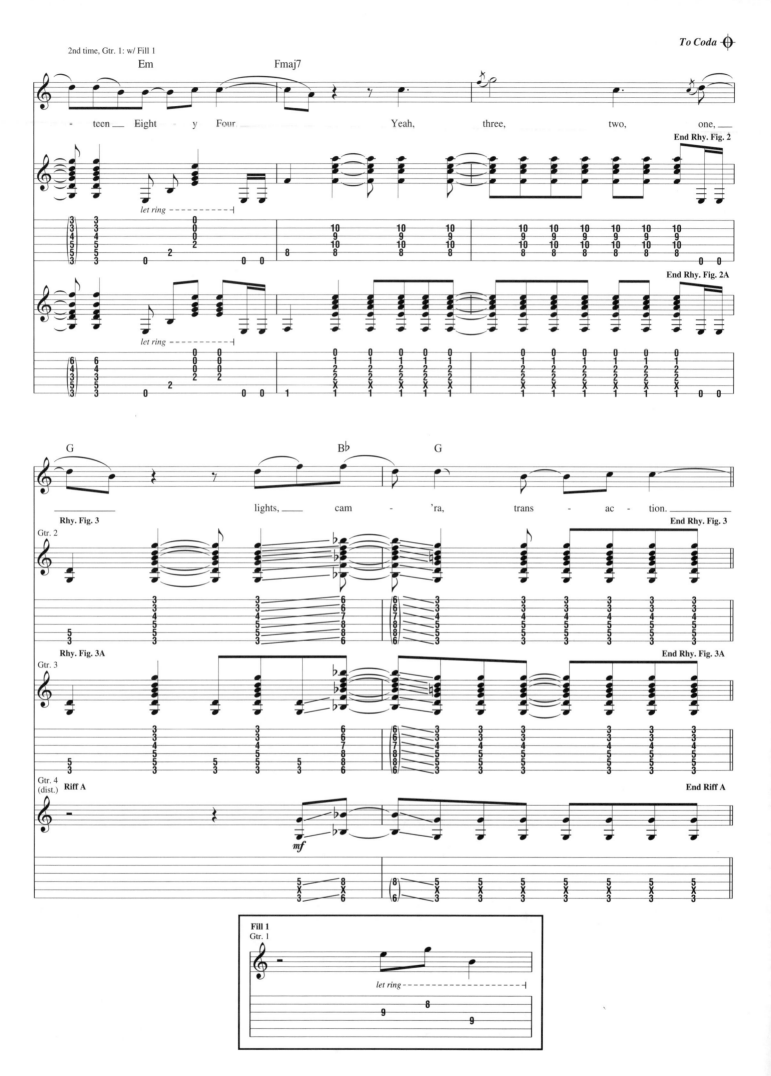

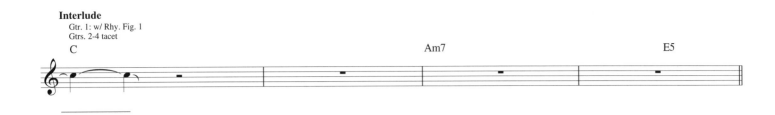

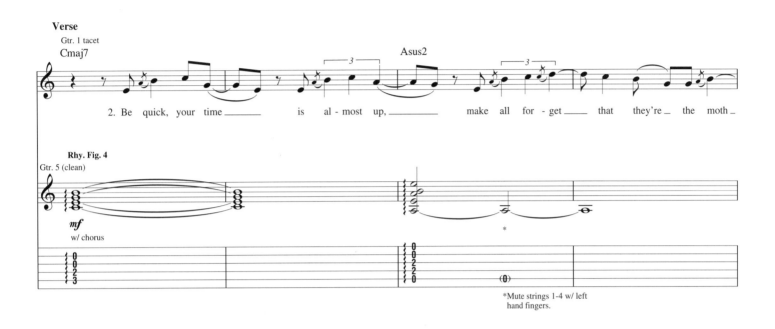

*Mute strings 1-4 w/ left
hand fingers.

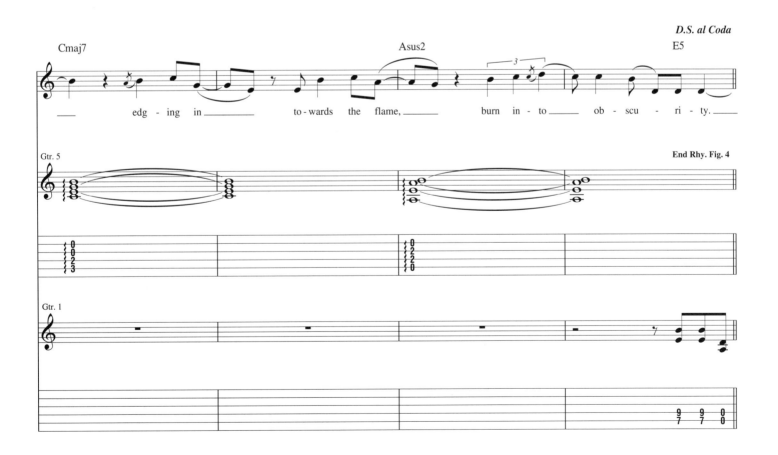

⊕ Coda

Gtrs. 2 & 3: w/ Rhy. Figs. 2 & 2A
Gtr. 4 tacet

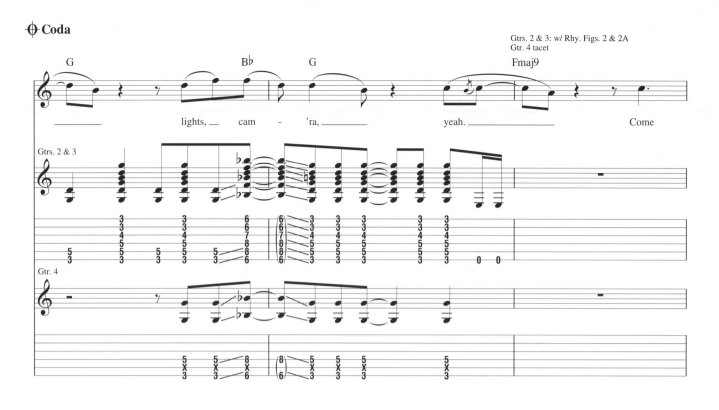

lights, _____ cam - 'ra, _____ yeah. _____ Come

one, come _ all _____ in - to Nine - teen _ Eight - y - Four. _____ Yeah,

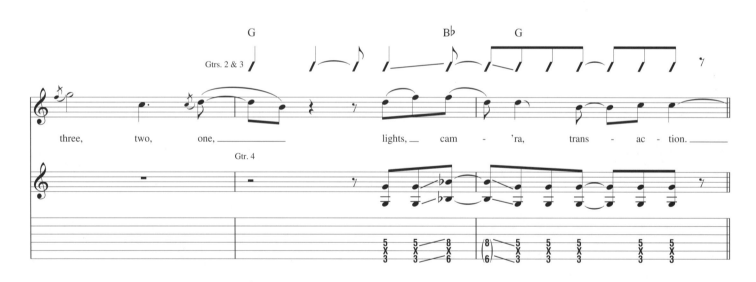

three, two, one, _____ lights, _____ cam - 'ra, trans - ac - tion. _____

Guitar Solo

*Gtr. 2: w/ Rhy. Fig. 4
Gtrs. 3 & 4 tacet

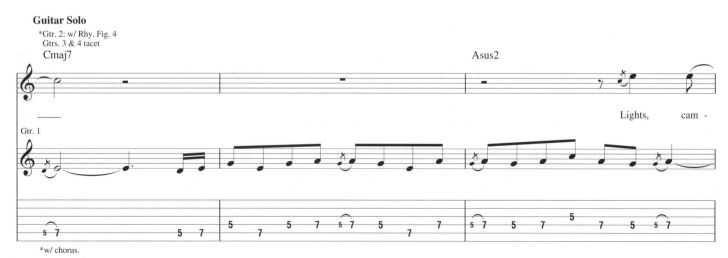

_____ Lights, cam -

*w/ chorus.

34

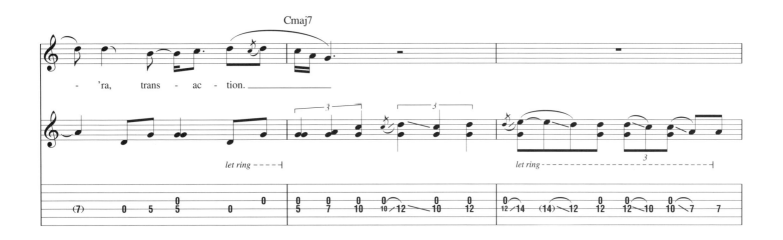

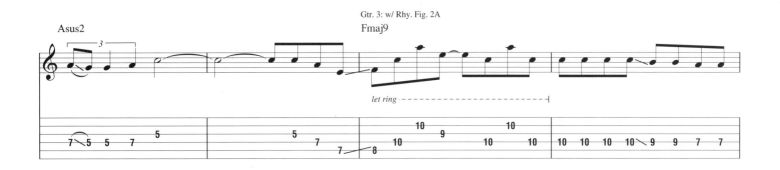

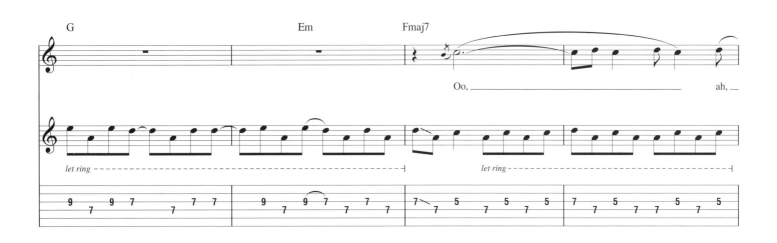

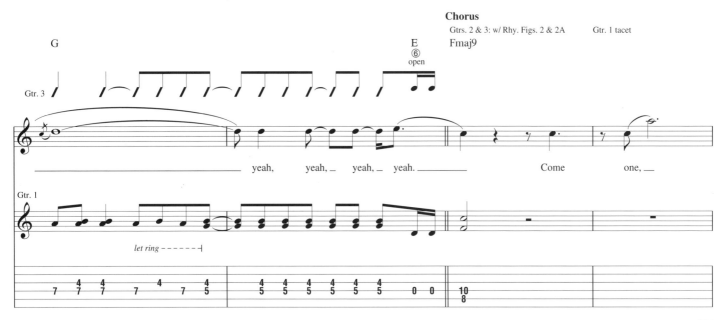

come ___ all ___ in-to Nine - teen ___ Eight - y Four. _____ Yeah, three, two, one, ____

Gtrs. 2 & 3: w/ Rhy. Figs. 3 & 3A
Gtr. 4: w/ Riff A

Interlude

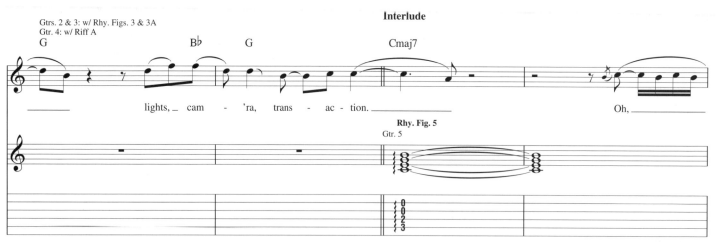

____ lights, __ cam - 'ra, trans - ac - tion. _____ Oh, _____

Rhy. Fig. 5
Gtr. 5

Verse
Gtr. 5: w/ Rhy. Fig. 5 (2 times)

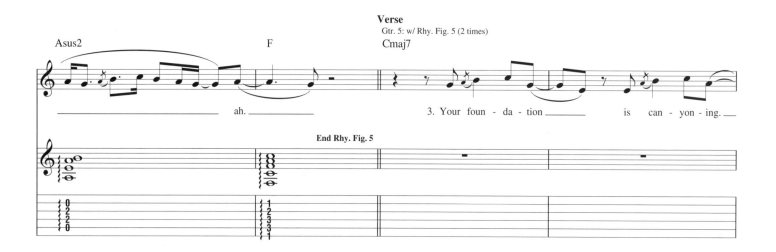

_____ ah. _____ 3. Your foun - da - tion _____ is can - yon - ing. ___

End Rhy. Fig. 5

_____ Fault lines should __ be __ worn __ with pride. ___ I hate to say it, but, so much more, ___

Outro
Free time

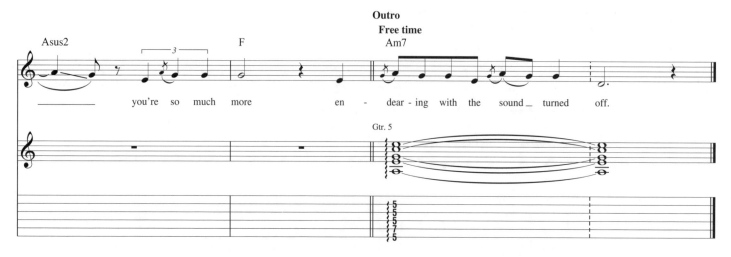

_____ you're so much more en - dear - ing with the sound __ turned off.

Gtr. 5

Beware! Criminal

Words and Music by Brandon Boyd, Michael Einziger, Jose Pasillas II, Chris Kilmore and Ben Kenney

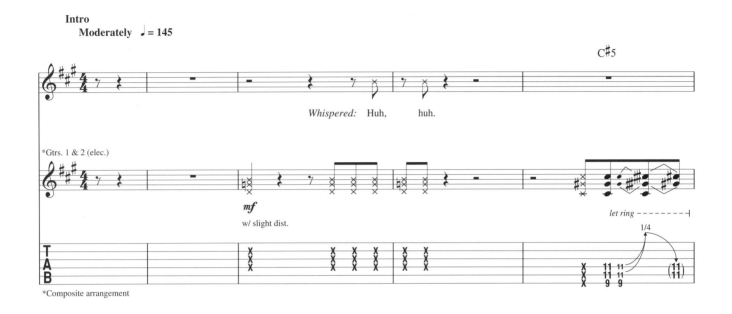

*Composite arrangement

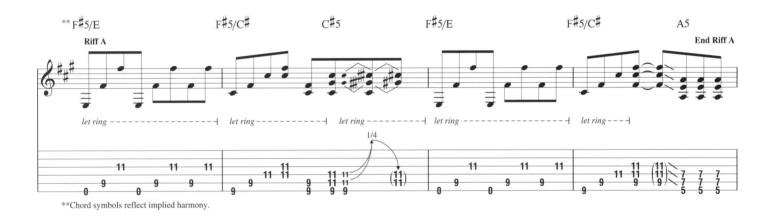

**Chord symbols reflect implied harmony.

Verse

_____ in bed, _____ it's three _____ a. m. _____ You smell of wine _____ and

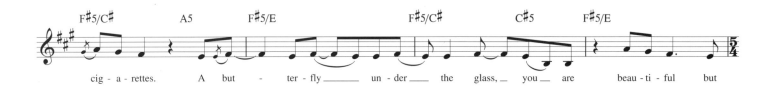

cig - a - rettes. A but - ter - fly _____ un - der _____ the glass, _____ you are beau - ti - ful but

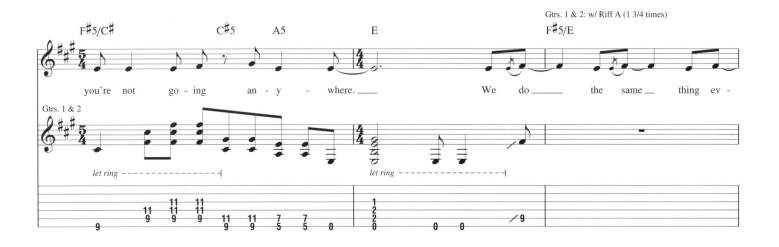

you're not go - ing an - y - where. _____ We do _____ the same _____ thing ev -

- 'ry night. _____ I swear I've heard _____ this song be - fore. _____ A swim -

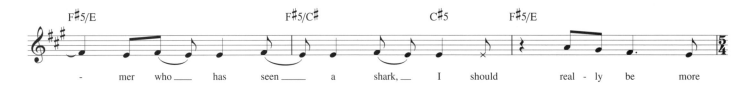

- mer who _____ has seen _____ a shark, _____ I should real - ly be more

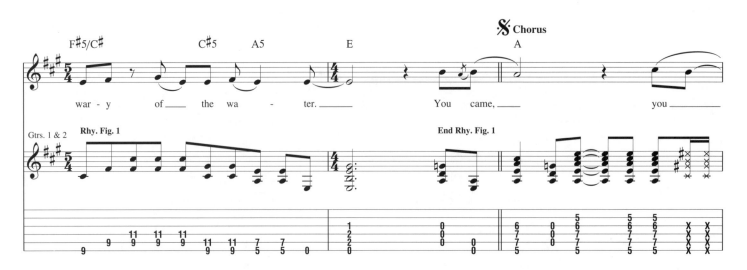

war - y of the wa - ter. _____ You came, _____ you _____

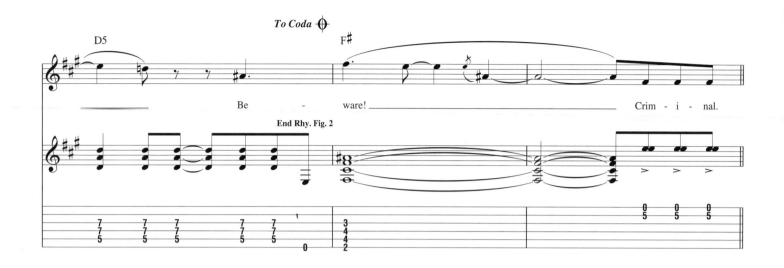

Be - ware! _____ Crim - i - nal.

Interlude

Crim -

- i - nal. _____ Oh, _____ Lord.

Verse

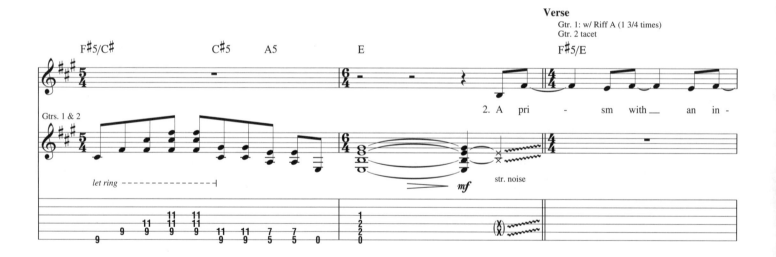

2. A pri - sm with _ an in -

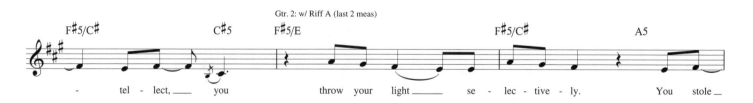

- tel - lect, _ you   throw your light _ se - lec - tive - ly.   You stole _

_ my glow, _ a sea - soned thief. The blacks _ of my eyes are

Interlude

*Doubled throughout

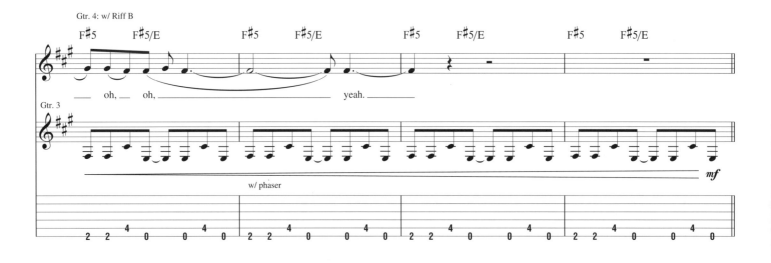

Bridge

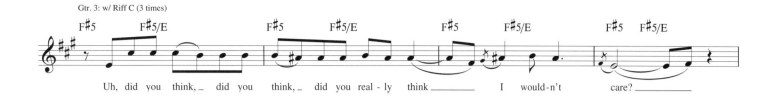

Gtr. 3: w/ Riff C (3 times)

F#5   F#5/E   F#5   F#5/E   F#5   F#5/E   F#5   F#5/E

Uh, did you think,_ did you think,_ did you real-ly think _____ I would-n't _____ care? _____

F#5   F#5/E   F#5   F#5/E   F#5   F#5/E   F#5   F#5/E

Uh, did you think,_ did you think _ I would - n't   no -   tice? _____

Gtr. 4 tacet

F#5   F#5/E   F#5   F#5/E   F#5   F#5/E   F#5   F#5/E

Uh, did you think, did you think, did you real - ly   think? ___   Yeah, _____ you   came, _

Gtr. 4

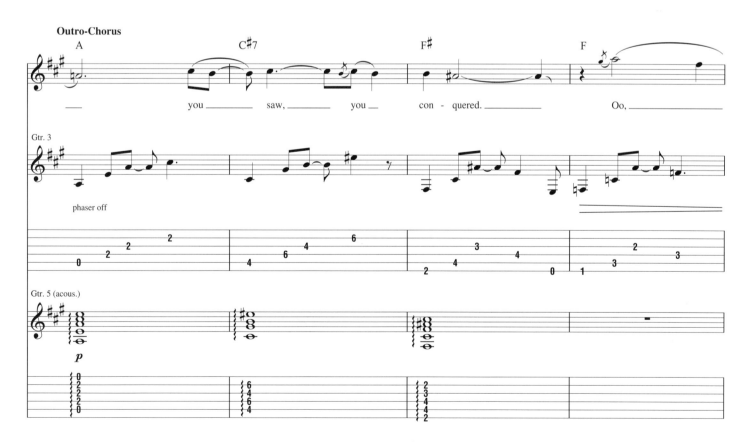

Outro-Chorus

A   C#7   F#   F

___ you _____ saw, _____ you ___ con - quered. _____   Oo, _____

Gtr. 3

phaser off

Gtr. 5 (acous.)

p

43

and I'm ___ left ___ here ___ bleed - ing. Oh, ___ what went ___

wrong? ___ Yeah, I'm down ___ but not out, ___ and ___

far from done. ___ Hey all! ___ Be -

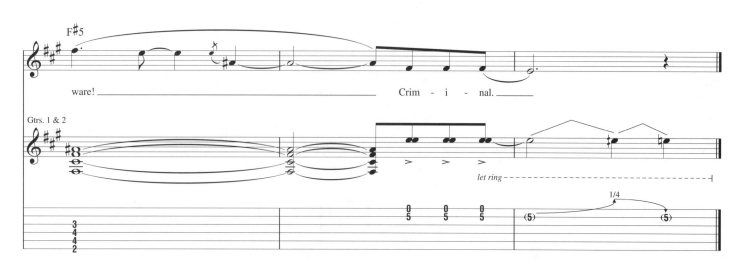

ware! ___ Crim - i - nal. ___

Sick Sad Little World

Words and Music by Brandon Boyd, Michael Einziger, Jose Pasillas II, Chris Kilmore and Ben Kenney

Intro
Moderately fast ♩ = 153

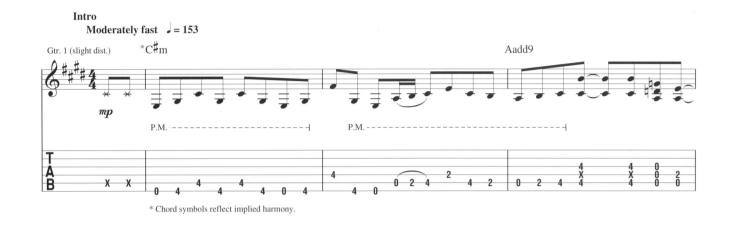

* Chord symbols reflect implied harmony.

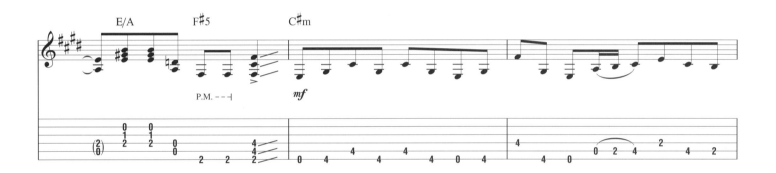

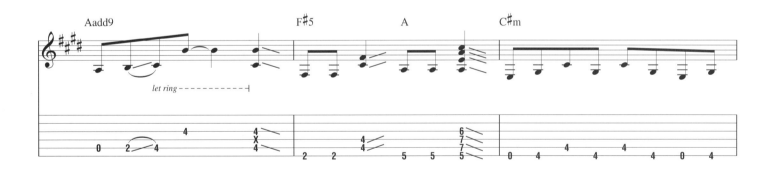

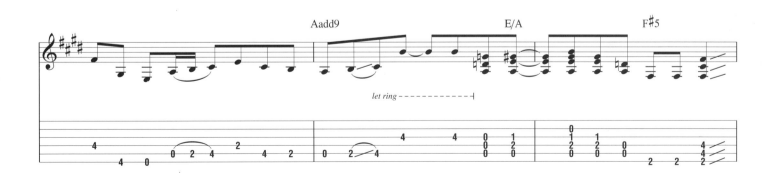

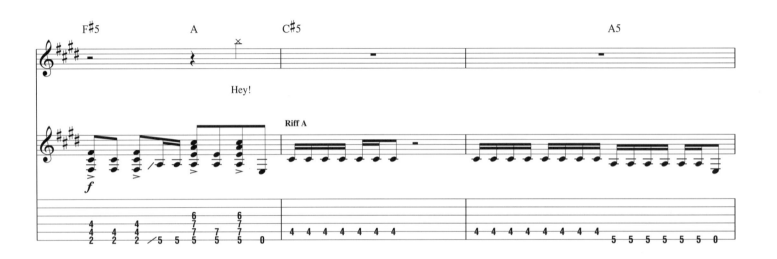

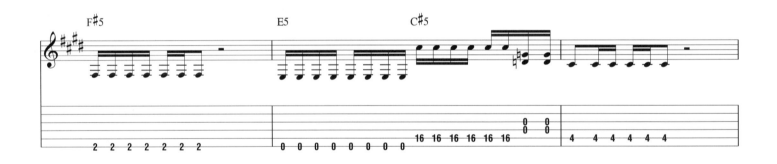

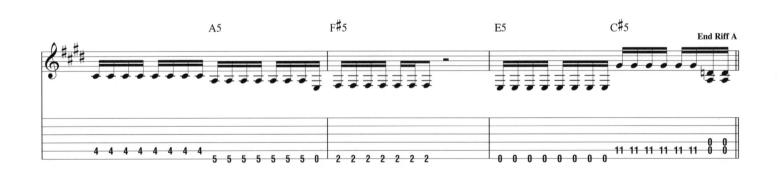

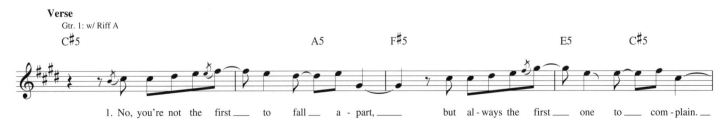

1. No, you're not the first ___ to fall ___ a - part, ___ but al - ways the first ___ one to ___ com - plain.

You bet-ter get care - ful or you'll com-pro-mise ev-'ry-thing __ you are. __

𝄋 Pre-Chorus
Half-time feel
2nd time, Gtr. 1 tacet

The world is a { drought __ / joke __ } when out __ of love.

*Gtr. 2
Rhy. Fig. 1
mf

*Piano arr. for gtr.

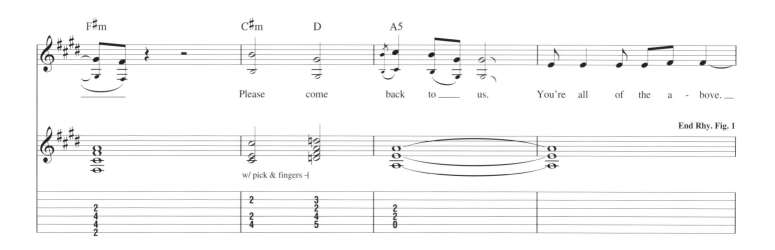

Please come back to __ us. You're all of the a - bove. __

End Rhy. Fig. 1

w/ pick & fingers

Gtr. 2: w/ Rhy. Fig. 1

"I'm mak-ing the choice __ to be out of touch. __

End half-time feel

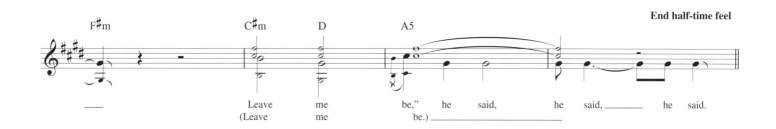

Leave me be," he said, he said, __ he said.
(Leave me be.) __

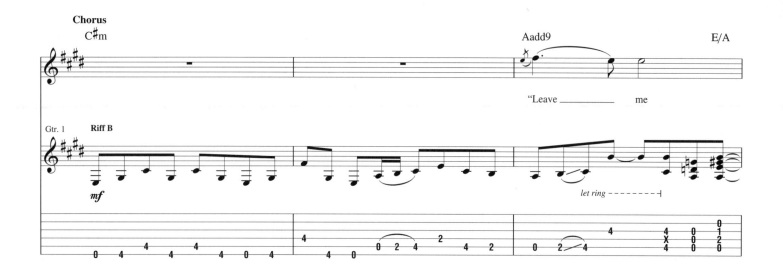

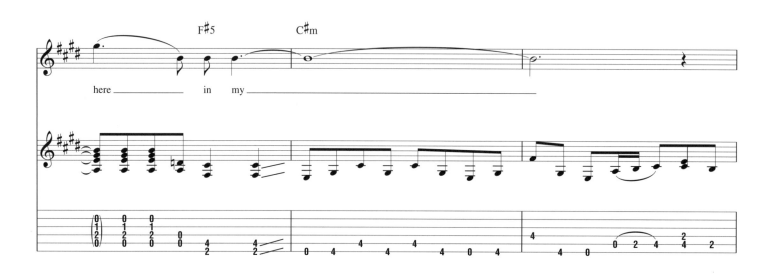

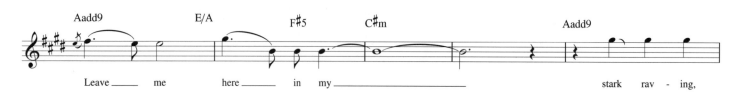

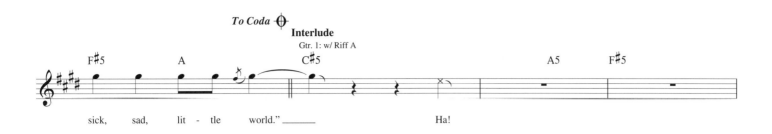

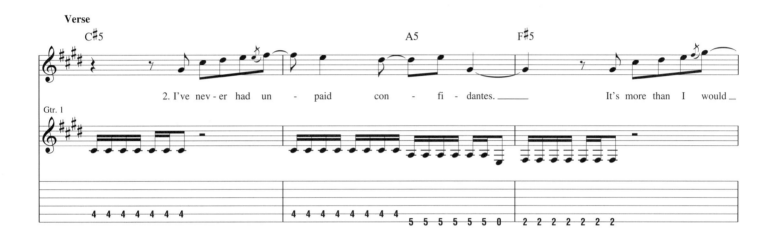

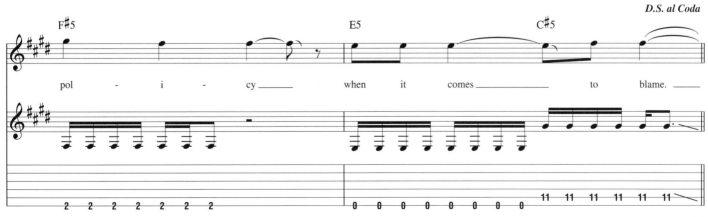

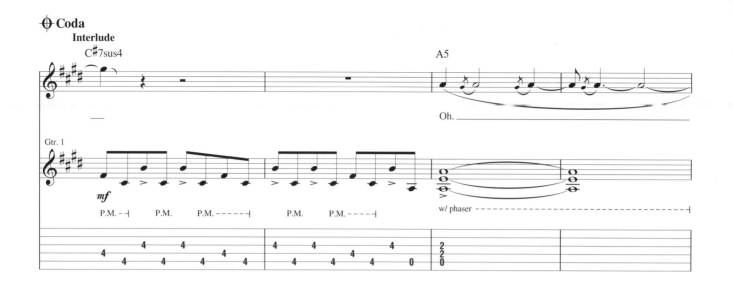

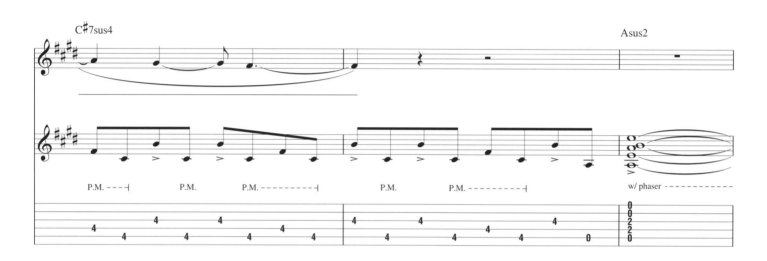

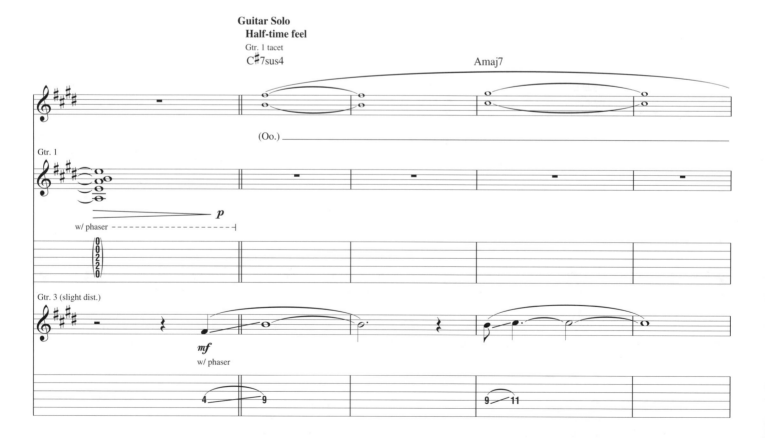

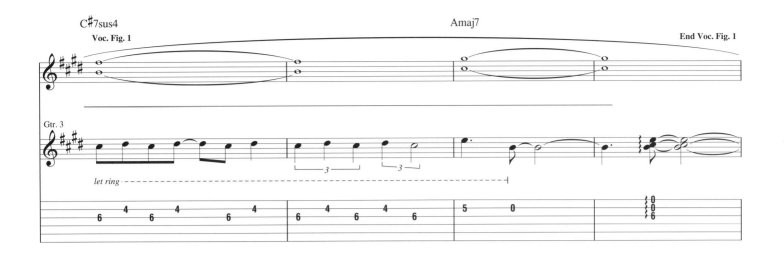

Bkgd. Voc: w/ Voc. Fig. 1 (6 times)

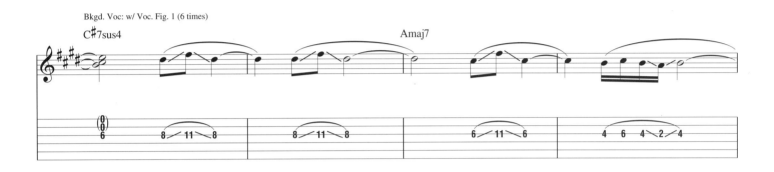

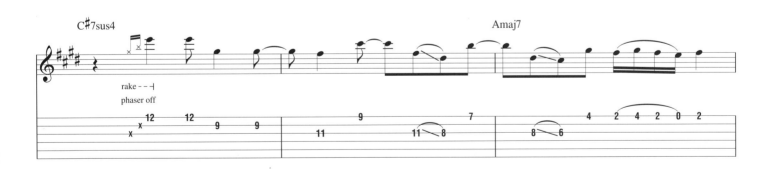

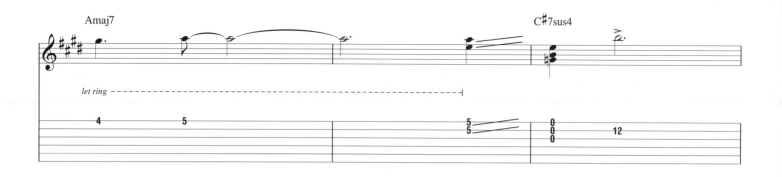

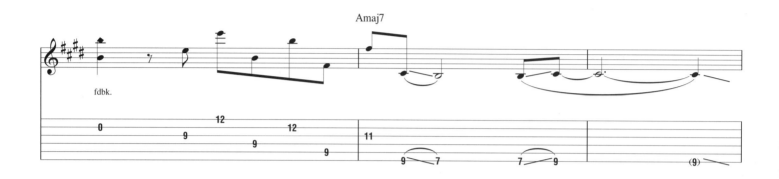

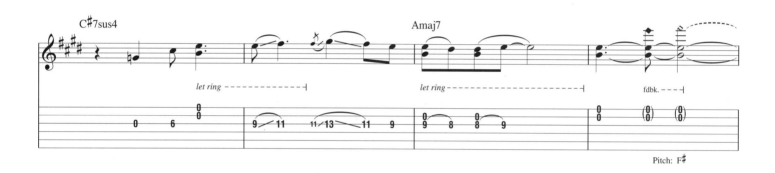

Pitch: F#

Gtr. 3 tacet

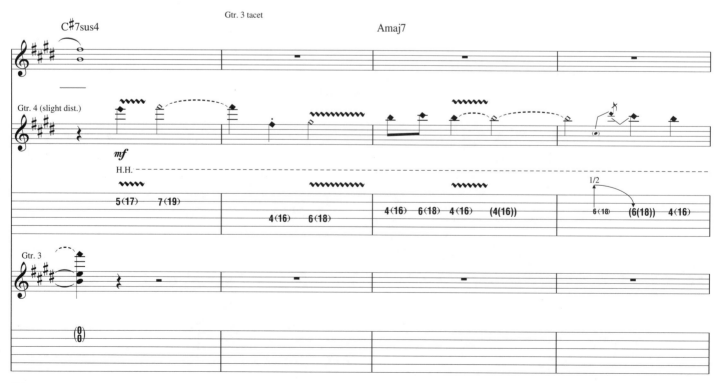

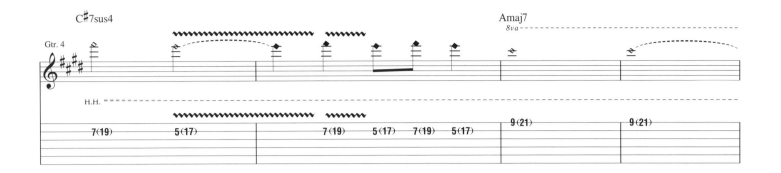

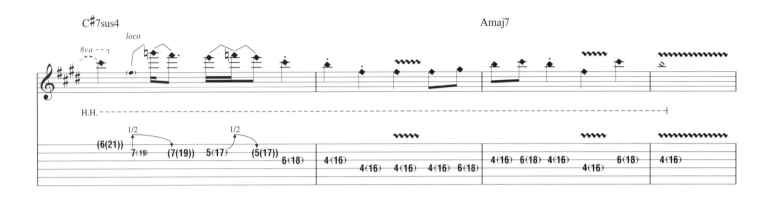

*Set flanger for slow sweep & delay for whole note regeneration w/ one repeat.

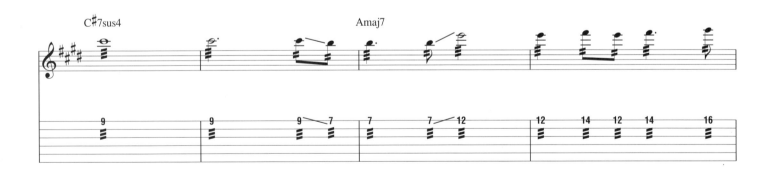

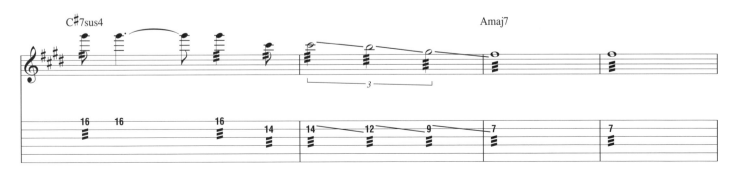

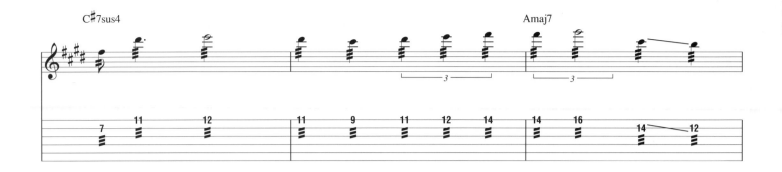

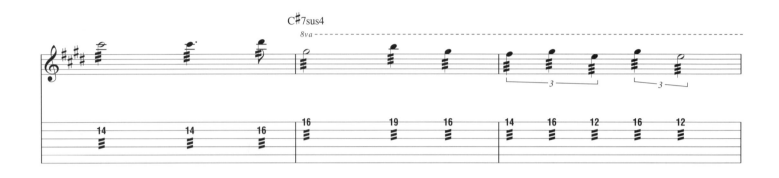

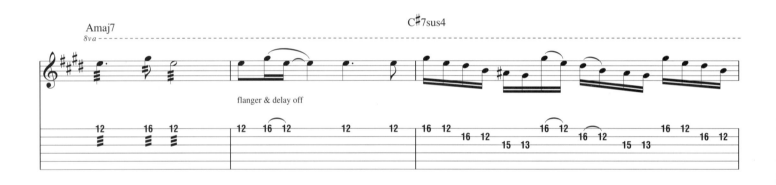

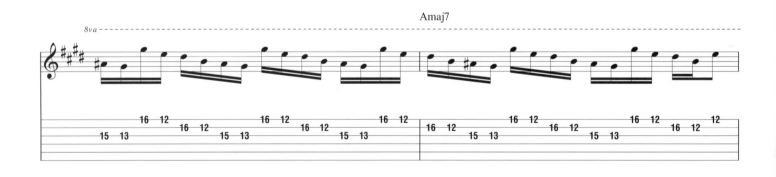

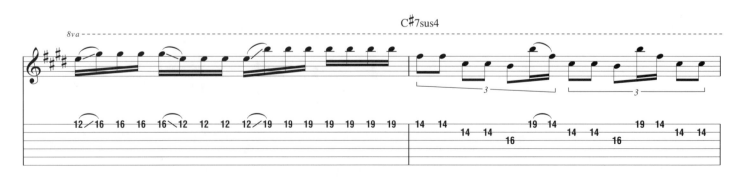

Interlude

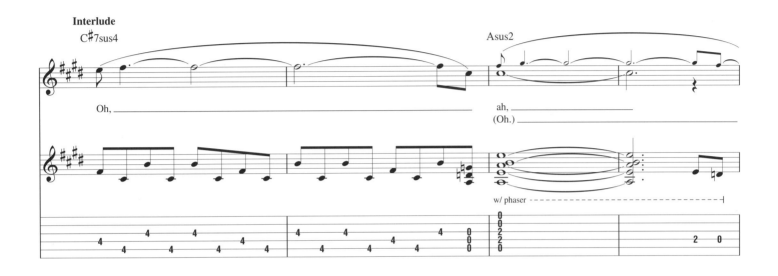

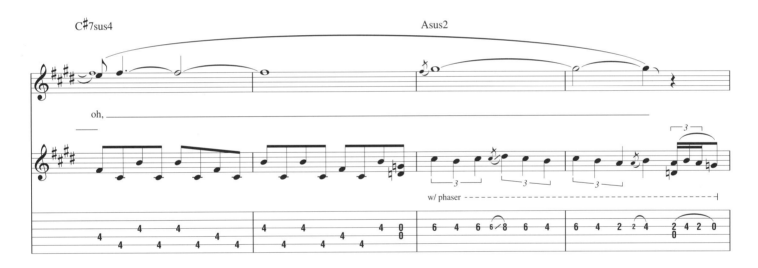

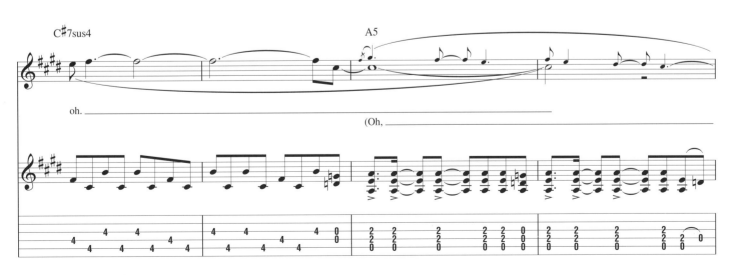

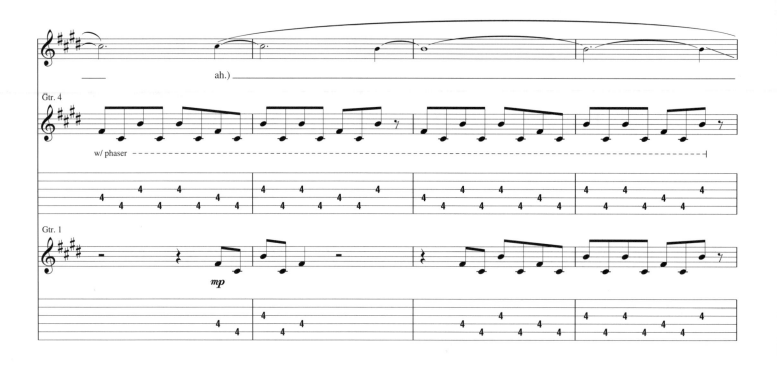

ah.)

Gtr. 4

w/ phaser

Gtr. 1

mp

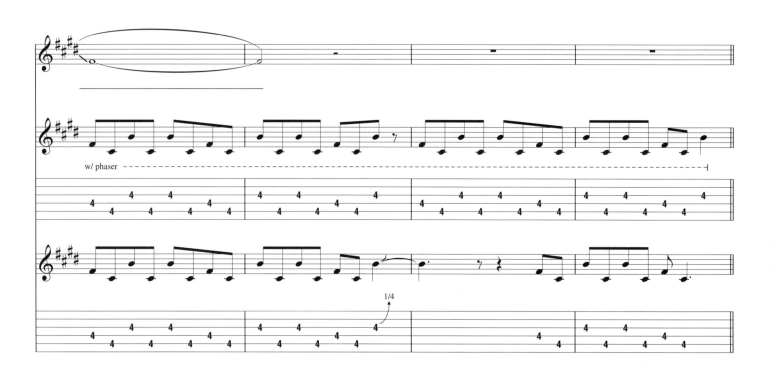

w/ phaser

1/4

Chorus

Gtr. 1: w/ Riff B (2 3/4 times)
Gtr. 4 tacet

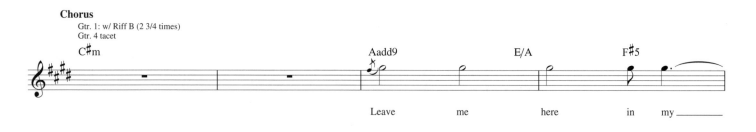

C#m   Aadd9   E/A   F#5

Leave   me   here   in   my_____

Gtr. 4: w/ Riff B (last 4 meas.)

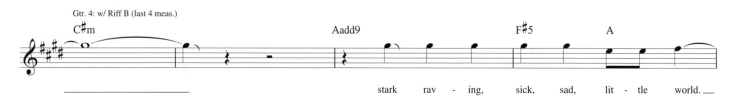

C#m   Aadd9   F#5   A

_____   stark   rav -   ing,   sick,   sad,   lit - tle   world. __

Gtr. 4: w/ Riff B (1 3/4 times)

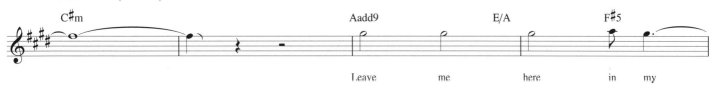

Leave me here in my

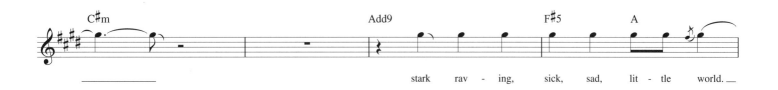

stark rav - ing, sick, sad, lit - tle world. __

_____

Oo. __

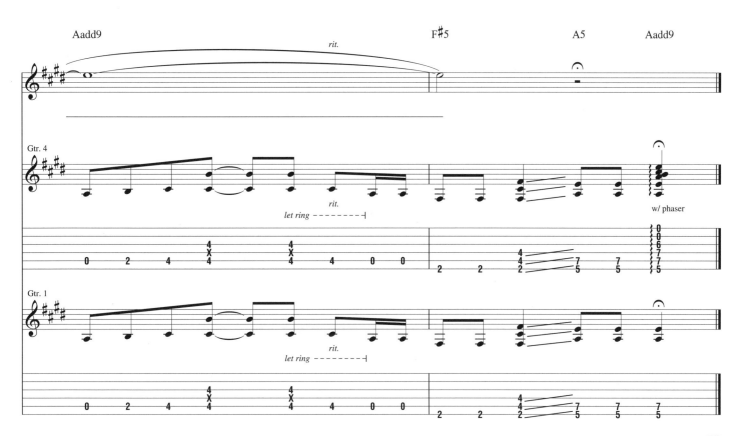

let ring --------|

w/ phaser

let ring --------|

Pistola

Words and Music by Brandon Boyd, Michael Einziger, Jose Pasillas II, Chris Kilmore and Ben Kenney

*Chord symbols reflect implied harmony.

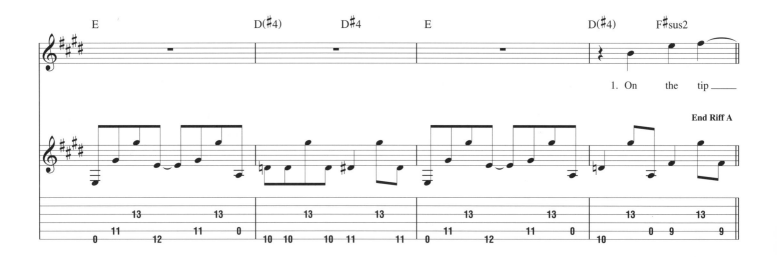

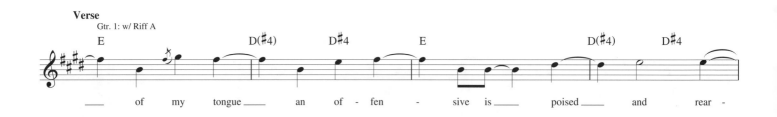

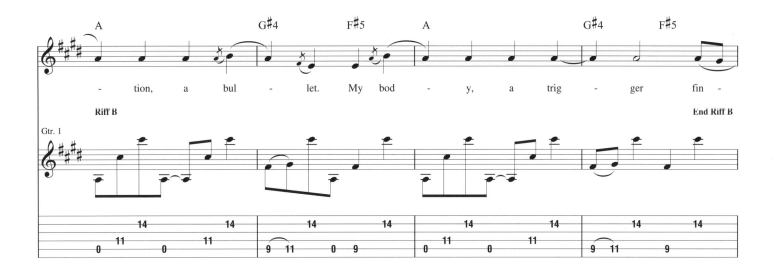

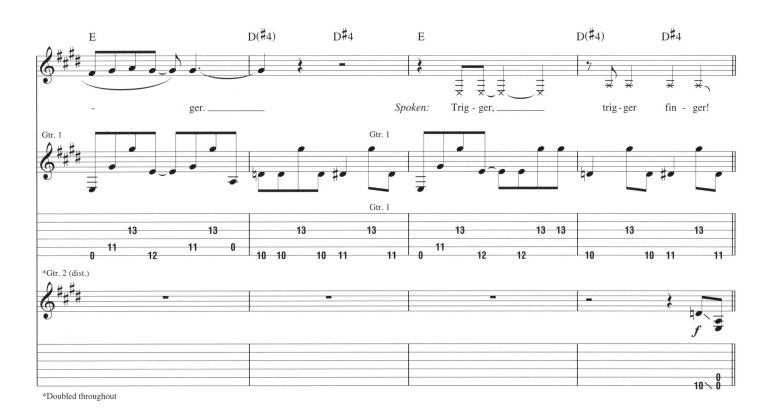

*Doubled throughout

**Composite arrangement

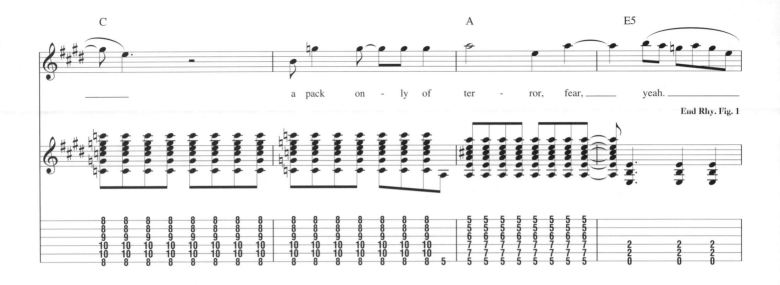

a pack on - ly of ter - ror, fear, _____ yeah. _____

End Rhy. Fig. 1

Gtrs. 2 & 3: w/ Rhy. Fig. 1

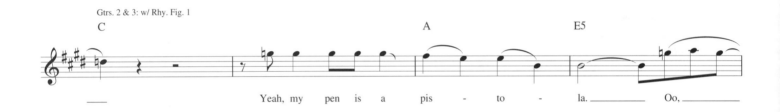

_____ Yeah, my pen is a pis - to - la. _____ Oo, _____

_____ oo, _____ oo. _____ 2. My se - cret _____

Verse

Gtr. 1: w/ Riff A

_____ ar - se - nal _____ is an in - fi - nite, age - less ink -

- well. _____ It's a foun -

Gtr. 1: w/ Riff B

- tain of _____ youth _____ and a pa - tri - ot's _____ weap - on of _____

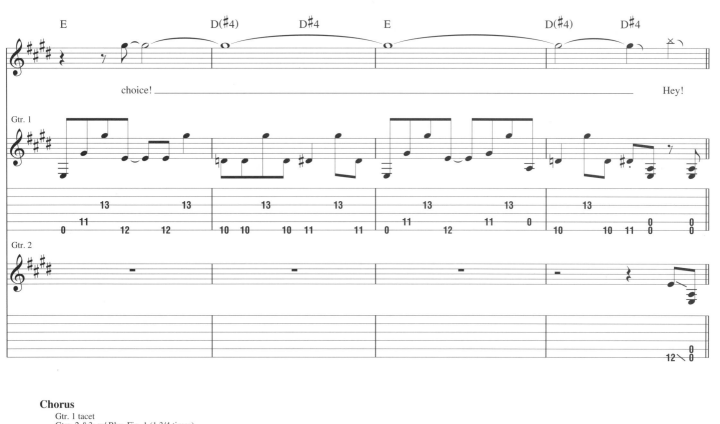

Chorus

Gtr. 1 tacet
Gtrs. 2 & 3: w/ Rhy. Fig. 1 (1 3/4 times)

Yeah, my pen is a pis - to - la. _____ Oo, _____

_____ a pack on - ly of ter - ror, fear, _____ yeah. _____

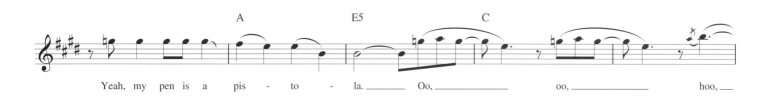

Yeah, my pen is a pis - to - la. _____ Oo, _____ oo, _____ hoo, _____

Interlude

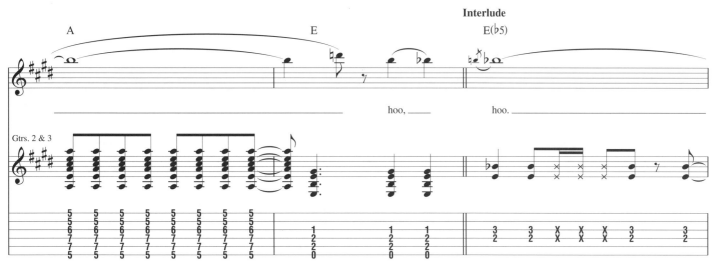

hoo, _____ hoo. _____

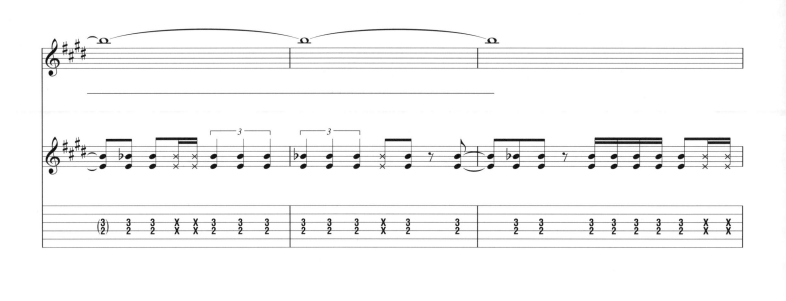
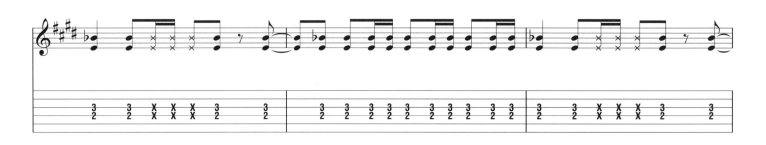
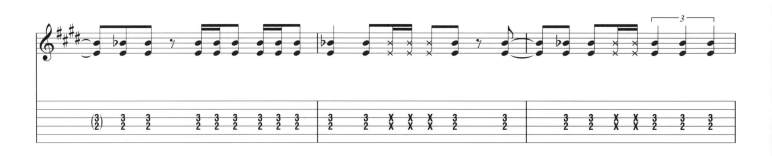
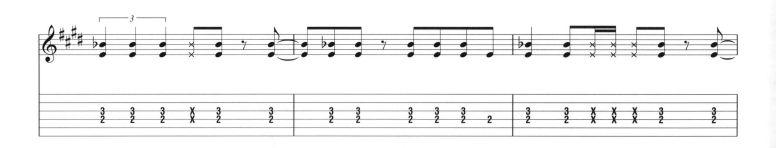
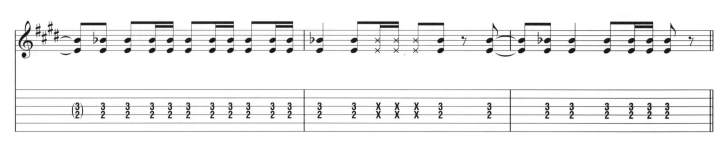

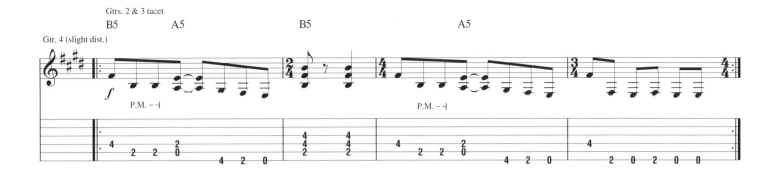

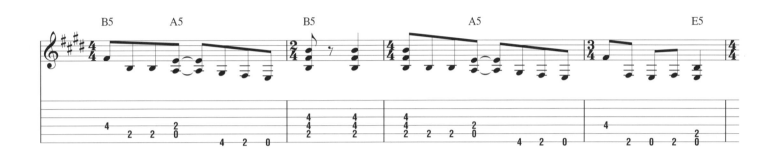

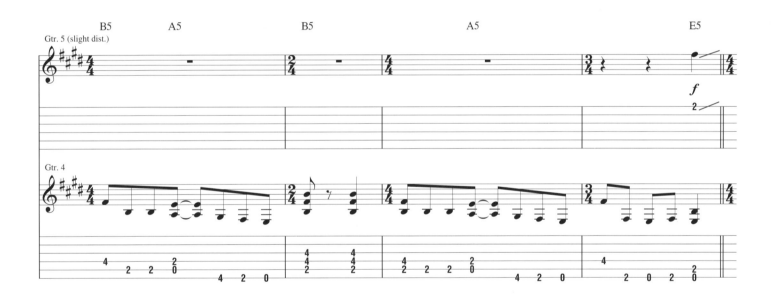

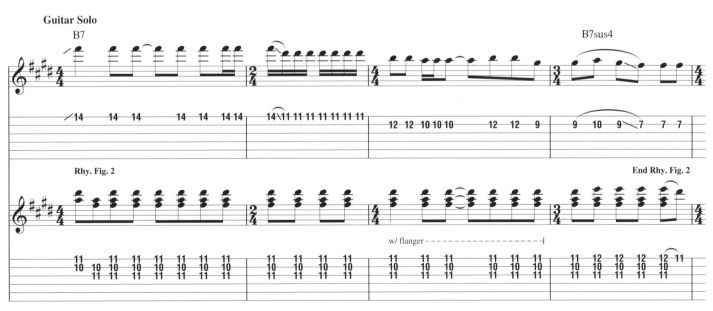

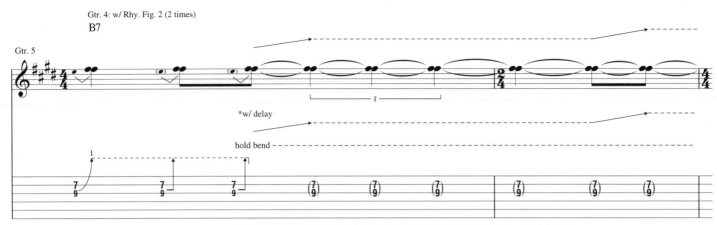

Gtr. 4: w/ Rhy. Fig. 2 (2 times)

*w/ delay

*Delay speed is controlled using foot pedal (toe down = speed increase, toe up = speed decrease).
Rhythm of tied notes indicates approximate delay speed. Arrows above notes indicate
acceleration/deceleration of delay speed (upward arrow = speed increase, downward arrow = speed decrease).

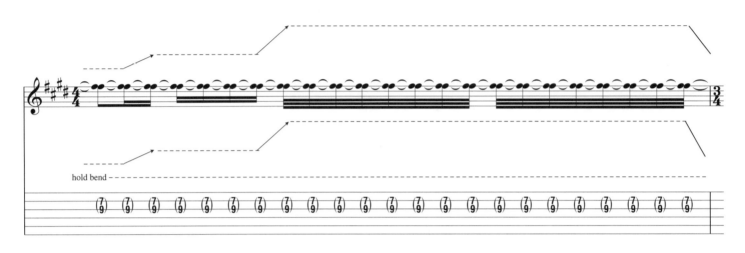

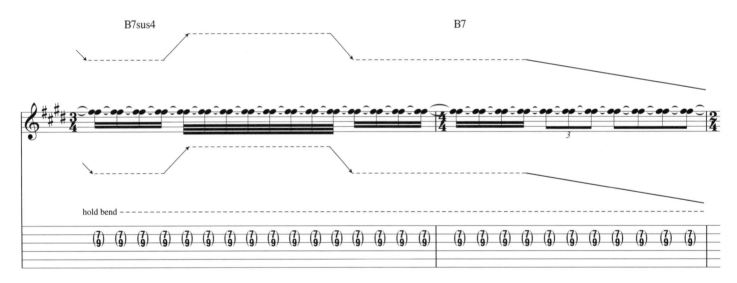

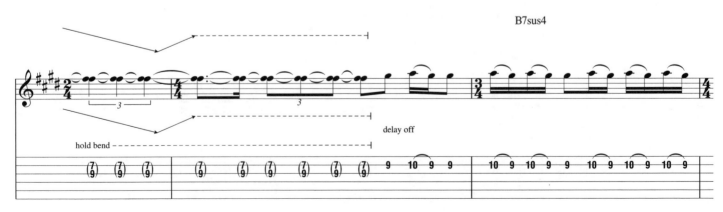

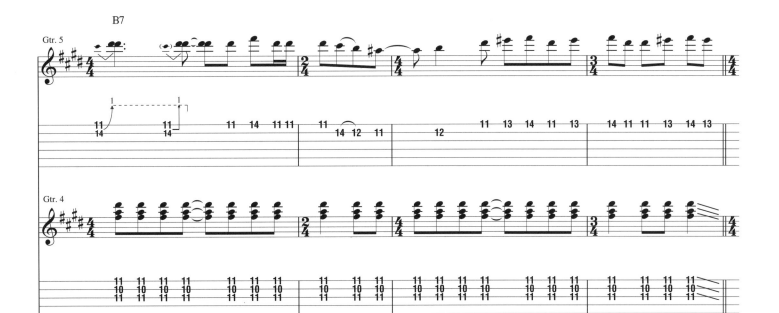

Interlude

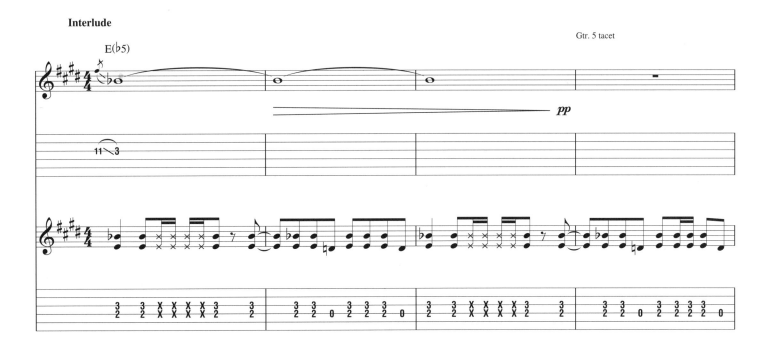

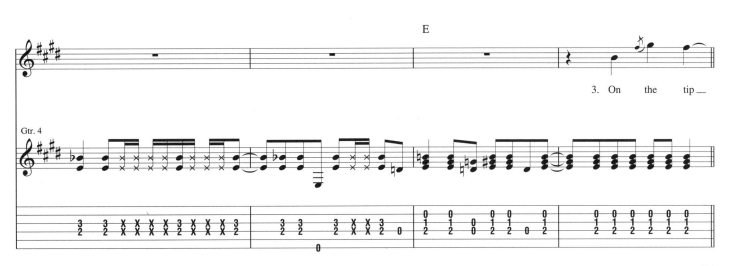

3. On the tip __

Verse

Gtr. 1: w/ Riff A (1 1/2 times)
Gtr. 4 tacet

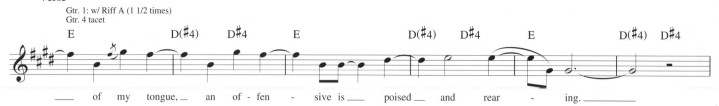

of my tongue,__ an of- fen - sive is__ poised__ and rear - ing.__

My in- ten - tion, a bul - let. My bod - y, a trig - ger fin -

Gtr. 1

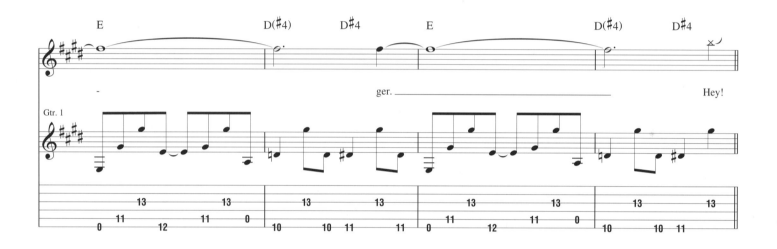

ger.__ Hey!

Chorus

Gtr. 1 tacet
Gtrs. 2 & 3: w/ Rhy. Fig. 1 (2 times)

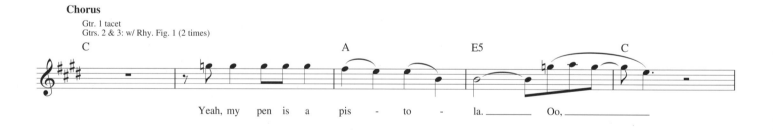

Yeah, my pen is a pis - to - la.__ Oo,__

a pack on - ly of fear.__ Yeah, my pen is a

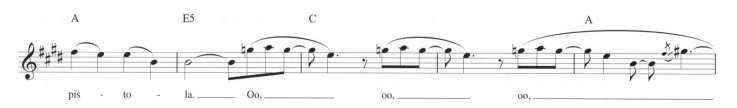

pis - to - la.__ Oo,__ oo,__ oo,__

Outro

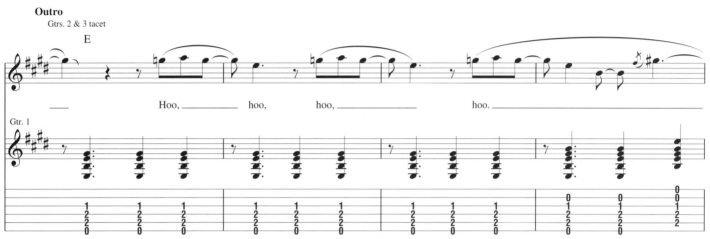

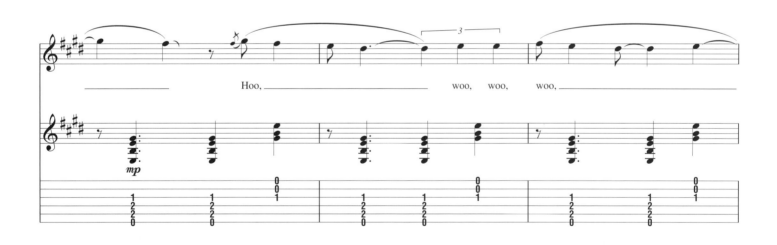

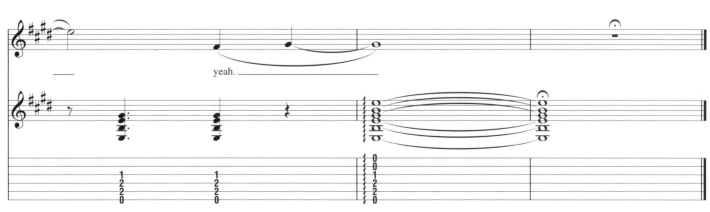

Southern Girl

Words and Music by Brandon Boyd, Michael Einziger, Jose Pasillas II, Chris Kilmore and Ben Kenney

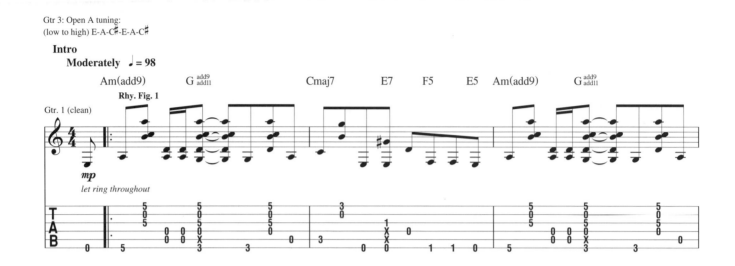

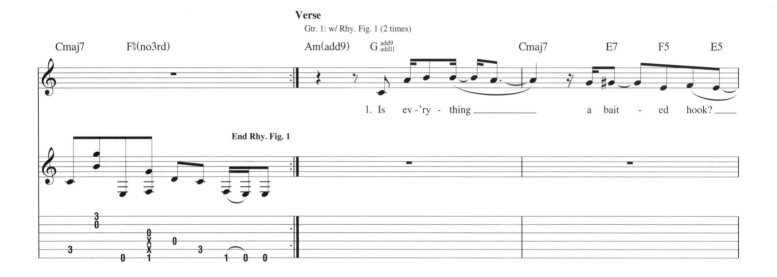

Pre-Chorus

We'll be-have ___ like ___ an - i - mals, ___ swing ___

Rhy. Fig. 2
Gtr. 1

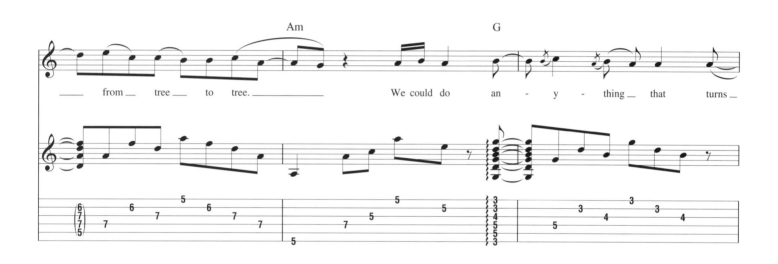

___ from ___ tree ___ to tree. ___ We could do an - y - thing ___ that turns ___

___ you up ___ and sets ___ you ___ free. ___

End Rhy. Fig. 2

*T = Thumb on 6th string

Chorus

Gtr. 1: w/ Rhy. Fig. 1 (1 1/2 times)

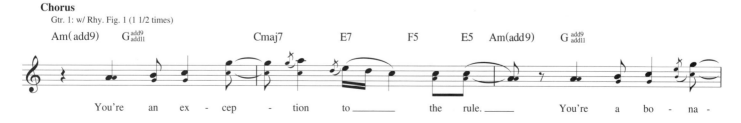

You're an ex-cep - tion to ___ the rule. ___ You're a bo - na -

-fide rar -i - ty.____ You're all I ev - er want - ed. South-

-ern girl,____ could you ____ want ____ me? ____

Gtr. 1 **Rhy. Fig. 3**

End Rhy. Fig. 3

Guitar Solo

Gtr. 1 tacet

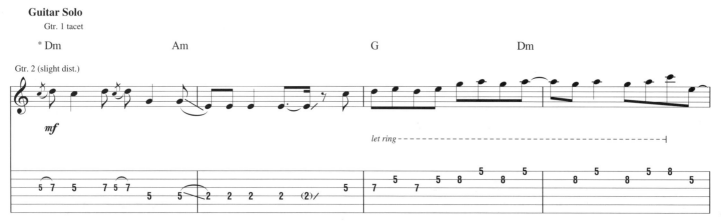

Gtr. 2 (slight dist.)

mf

let ring -

*Chord symbols reflect implied harmony.

let ring - - - - - - - - - - - - -

let ring - - -

Verse

Gtr. 1: w/ Rhy. Fig. 1 (2 times)
Gtr. 2 tacet

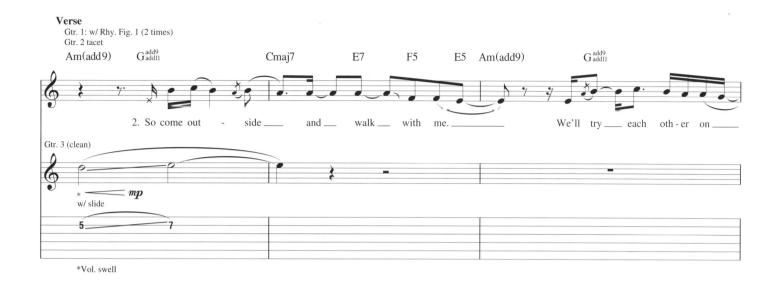

2. So come out - side ___ and ___ walk ___ with me. ___ We'll try ___ each oth - er on ___

Gtr. 3 (clean)

* *mp*

w/ slide

*Vol. swell

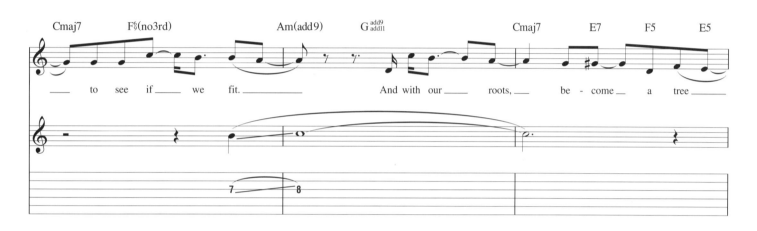

___ to see if ___ we fit. ___ And with our ___ roots, ___ be - come ___ a tree ___

Pre-Chorus

Gtr. 3 tacet

Gtr. 1: w/ Rhy. Fig. 2

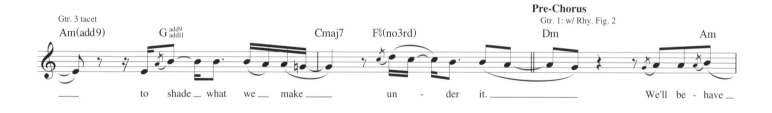

___ to shade ___ what we make ___ un - der it. ___ We'll be - have ___

___ like ___ an - i - mals, ___ swing ___ from ___ tree to tree.

Gtr. 3

___ We could do an - y - thing ___ that turns ___ you up ___ and sets ___

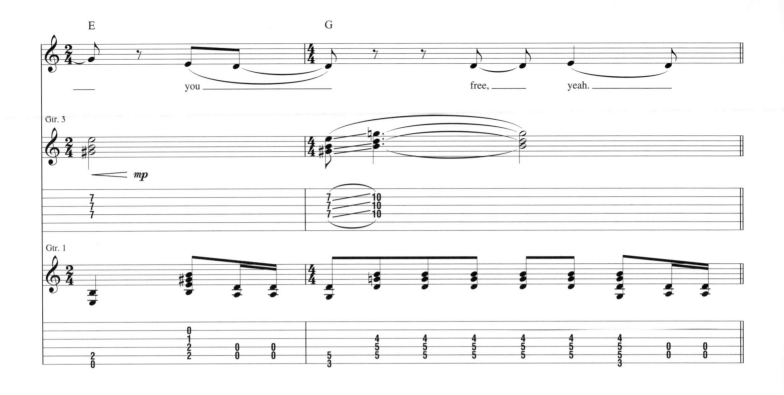

Chorus

Gtr. 1: w/ Rhy. Fig. 1 (1 1/2 times)
Gtr. 3 tacet

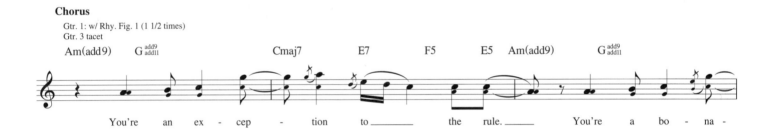

You're an ex - cep - tion to the rule. You're a bo - na -

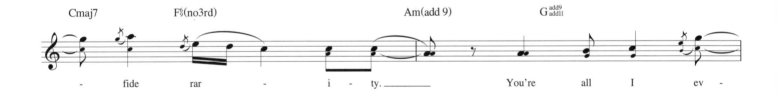

- fide rar - i - ty. You're all I ev -

Gtr. 1: w/ Rhy. Fig. 3

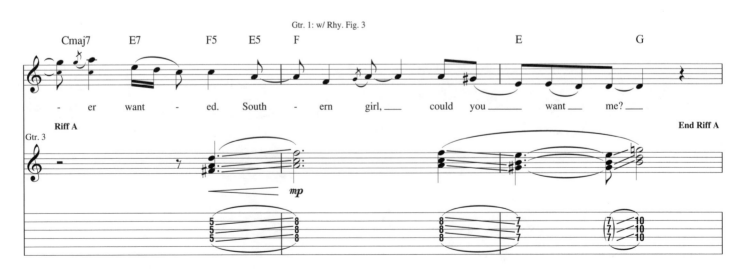

- er want - ed. South - ern girl, could you want me?

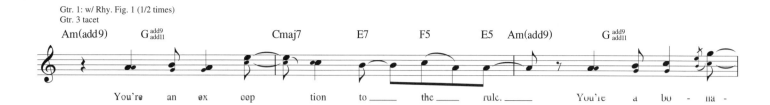

You're an ex - cep - tion to the rule. You're a bo - na -

- fide rar - i - ty. You're all I ev - er want - ed. South -

Outro

- ern girl, could you want me? South - ern girl, could you

want me? South - ern girl, could you want me? Could you want me?
(Could you want me?) Could you want me?

*Applies to upstemmed notes only.

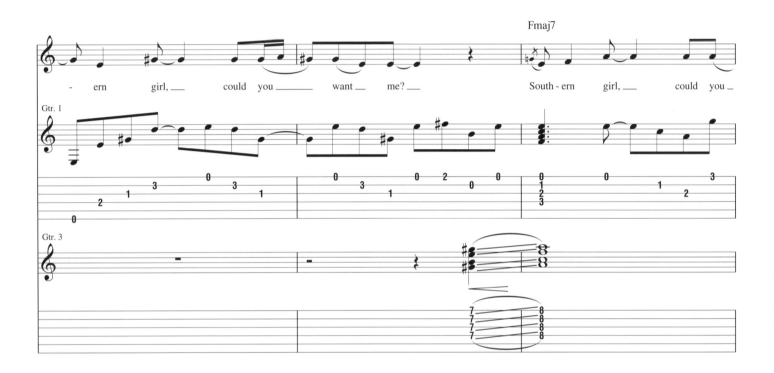

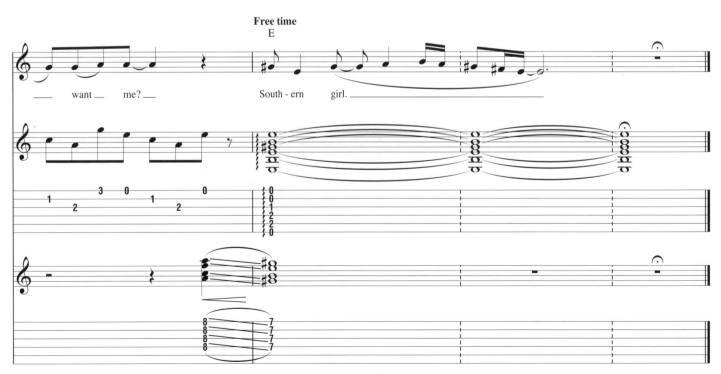

Priceless

Words and Music by Brandon Boyd, Michael Einziger, Jose Pasillas II, Chris Kilmore and Ben Kenney

Intro
Moderately fast ♩ = 178

Gtr. 1 (slight dist.)

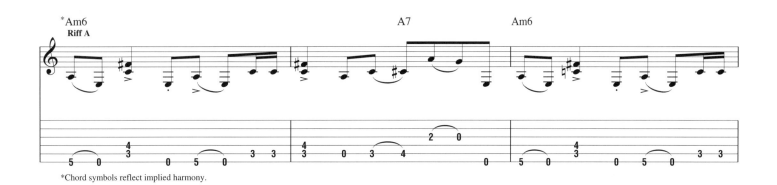

*Chord symbols reflect implied harmony.

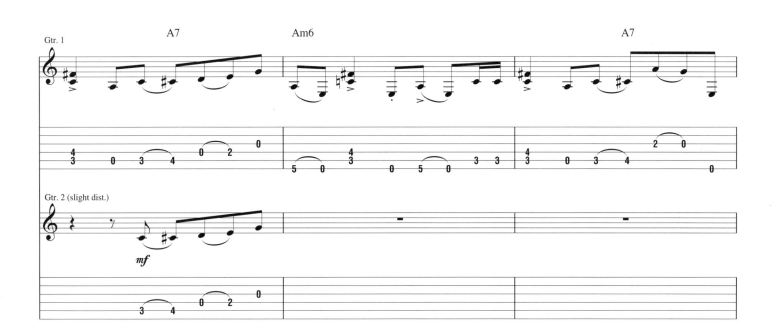

Gtrs. 1 & 2: w/ Riff A

Verse

speak to me the way you do, it

End Riff B

End Riff B1

Gtrs. 1 & 2: w/ Riffs B & B1 (2 1/2 times)

bleeds me to be - lieve that you have nev - er stepped __ out of the __

__ skin you live with - in. When and if this day oc - curs, your

tongue, the taste will im - i - tate a bat - ter - y, the

an - ti - e - qui - lib - ri - um. __ Your stom - ach be - comes __ the

Gtr. 1

Pre-Chorus

Gtrs. 1 & 2: w/ Riff A

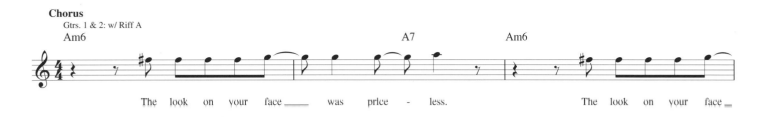

The look on your face____ was price - less. The look on your face____

____ was price - less. Yes, the look on your face____ was price - less.

Verse

Gtrs. 1 & 2: w/ Riffs B & B1 (2 times)

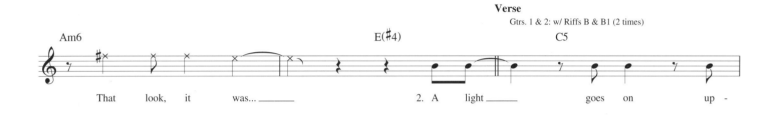

That look, it was... _____ 2. A light _____ goes on up -

stairs, the at - tic is a - blaze. This is - land is - n't

big e - nough for both of us. So who will swim in eel in - fest - ed o - ceans?

Kiss the sand good - bye be - cause the tide is com - ing up and in. Yeah,

Pre-Chorus

Gtrs. 1 & 2: w/ Rhy. Figs. 1 & 1A (3 times) Gtrs. 1 & 2: w/ Rhy. Figs. 2 & 2A

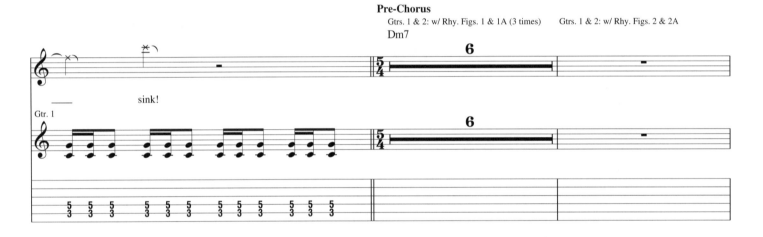

Chorus

Gtrs. 1 & 2: w/ Riff A

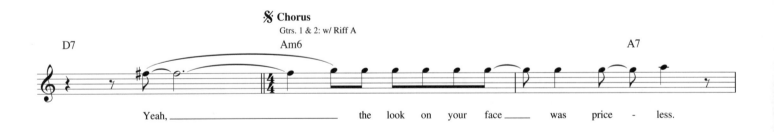

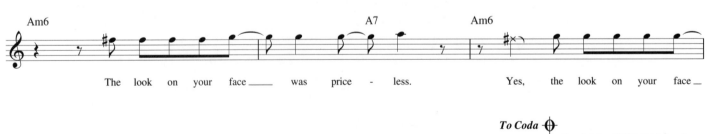

To Coda

Gtrs. 1 & 2: w/ Riff B (1 1/2 times)

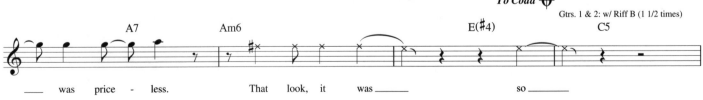

price - less, _____ price - less, _____ so _____

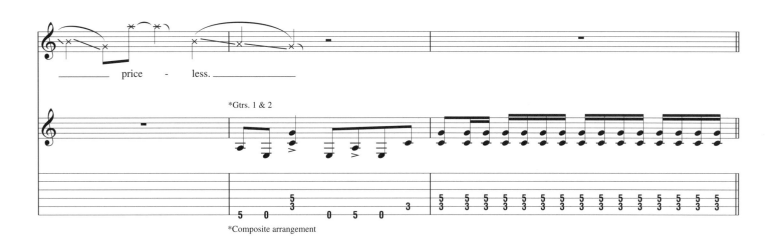

_____ price - less. _____

*Gtrs. 1 & 2

*Composite arrangement

Guitar Solo

Gtr. 2 tacet

N.C.

Gtr. 1

Am7

w/ heavy flanger

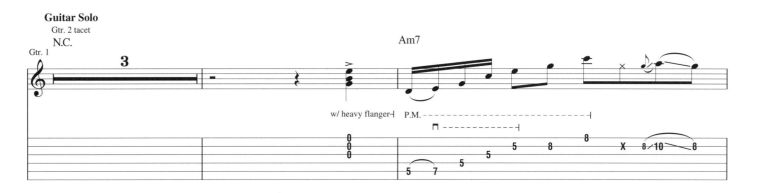

Cm

loco

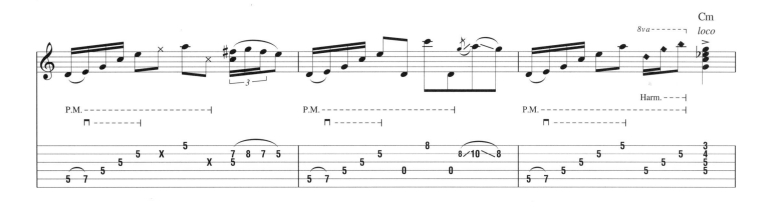

Am7

Cm   Am7

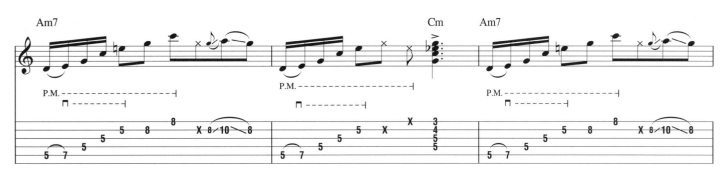

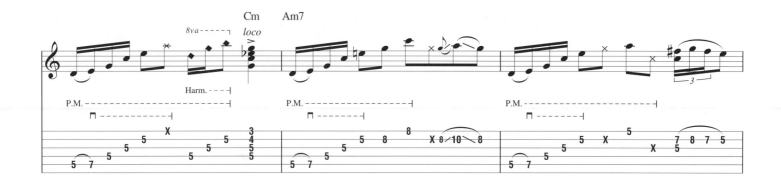

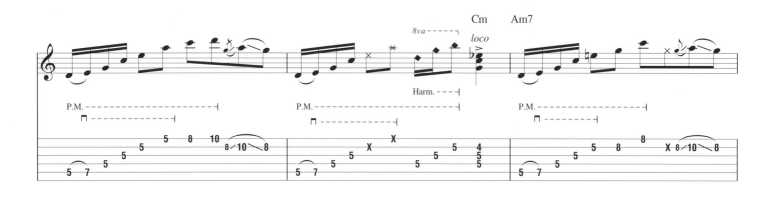

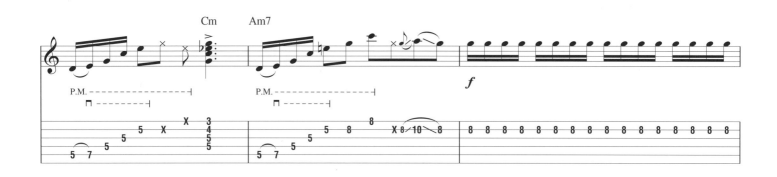

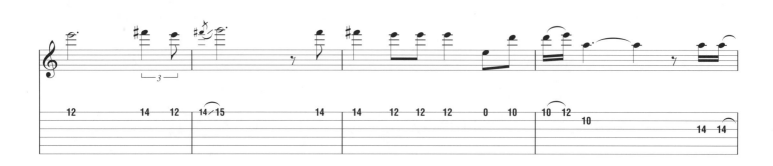

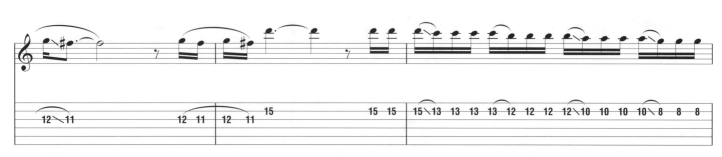

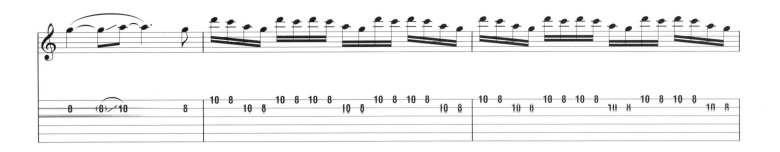

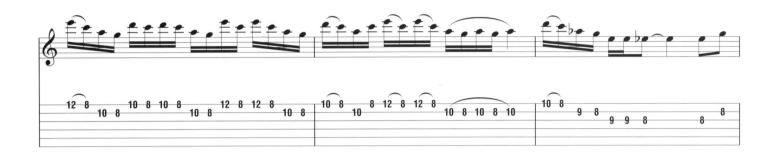

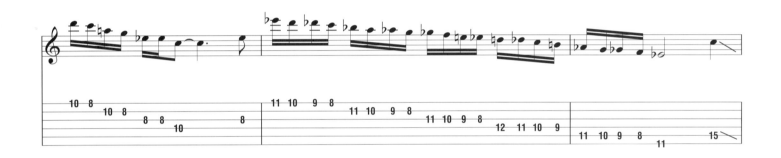

Half-time feel

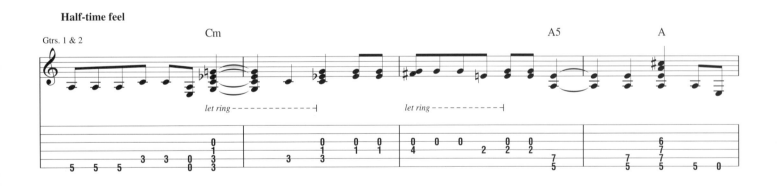

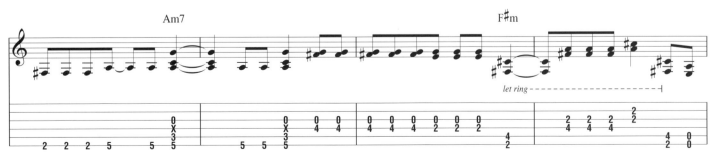

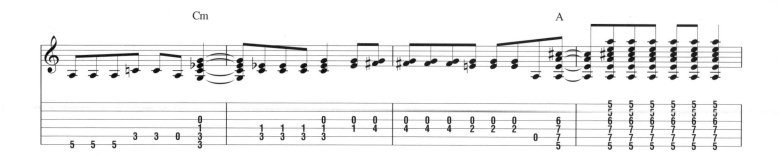

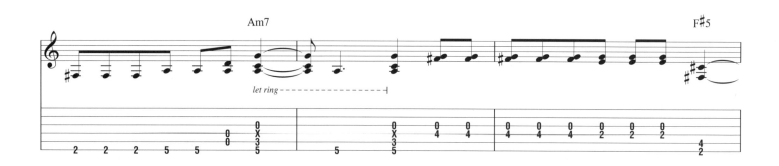

Verse
End half-time feel

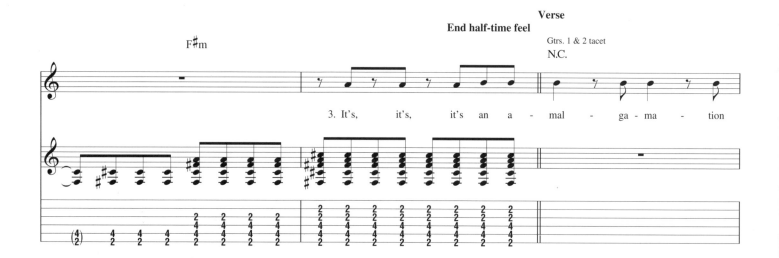

3. It's, it's, it's an a - mal - ga - ma - tion

of the things you aren't, the ways you wish you were. A

Gtr. 1: w/ Riff A (1st 6 meas.)

split sec - ond per - ceiv - ing of the way you real - ly look

to ev - 'ry - one of them. I wish that you could see be - cause I

84

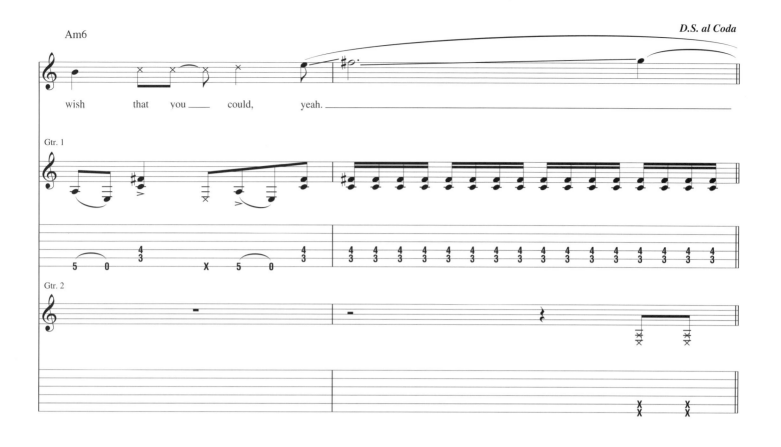

wish   that   you ____ could,   yeah. _____

Coda

___   price - less, _____ so _____ price -

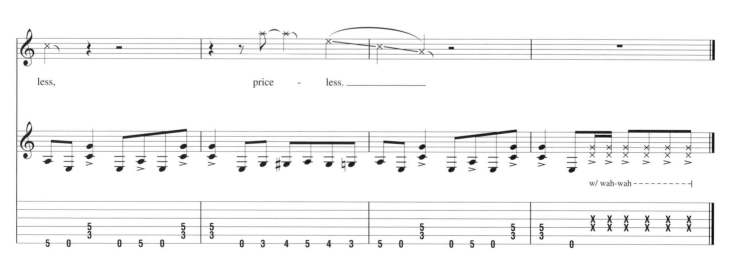

less,   price - less. _____

w/ wah-wah - - - - - - - -

Zee Deveel

Words and Music by Brandon Boyd, Michael Einziger, Jose Pasillas II, Chris Kilmore and Ben Kenney

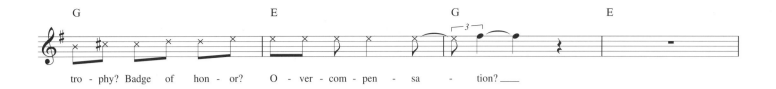

tro - phy? Badge of hon - or? O - ver - com - pen - sa - tion?

Price tags, ad - ver - tise your pride. Since

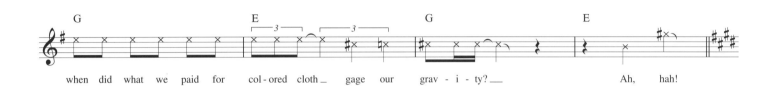

when did what we paid for col - ored cloth gage our grav - i - ty? Ah, hah!

𝄋 Pre-Chorus

Yeah, you got your lit - tle world. Pic - ture per - fect, it's a pearl.

Gtr. 1

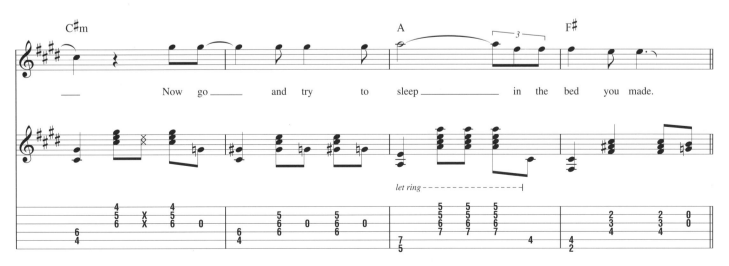

Now go and try to sleep in the bed you made.

let ring

Chorus

You should be care - ful what you wish for,

*Composite arrangement

Gtrs. 1 & 2: w/ Rhy. Fig. 2 (2 3/4 times)
2nd time, Bkgd. Voc.: w/ Voc. Fig. 1

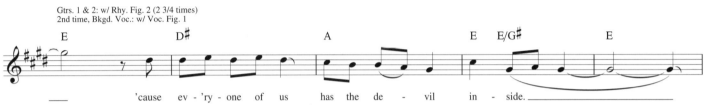

'cause ev - 'ry - one of us has the de - vil in - side.

2nd time, Bkgd. Voc.: w/ Voc. Fig. 2

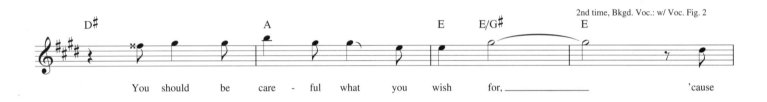

You should be care - ful what you wish for, _____ 'cause

To Coda ⊕

Gtrs. 1 & 2: w/ Rhy. Fill 1

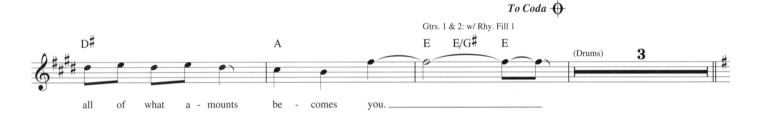

all of what a - mounts be - comes you. _____

Voc. Fig. 1

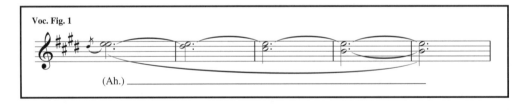

(Ah.) _____

Voc. Fig. 2

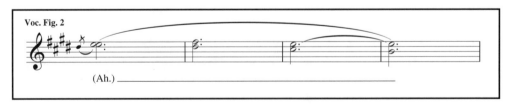

(Ah.) _____

Rhy. Fill 1
Gtrs. 1 & 2

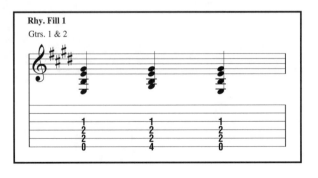

Interlude

Gtrs. 1 & 2: w/ Rhy. Fig. 1 (2 times)

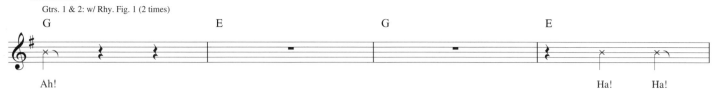

Ah!   Ha! Ha!

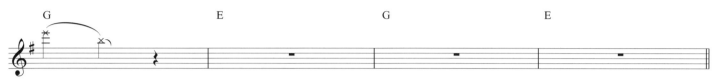

Whoo! _____

Verse

Gtr. 1: w/ Rhy. Fig. 1 (2 times)

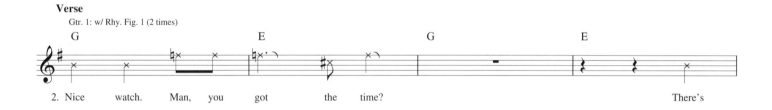

2. Nice watch. Man, you got the time?   There's

D. S. al Coda

nev - er e -nough and it al - ways goes too slow, _____   uh, too slow.

Coda

Interlude

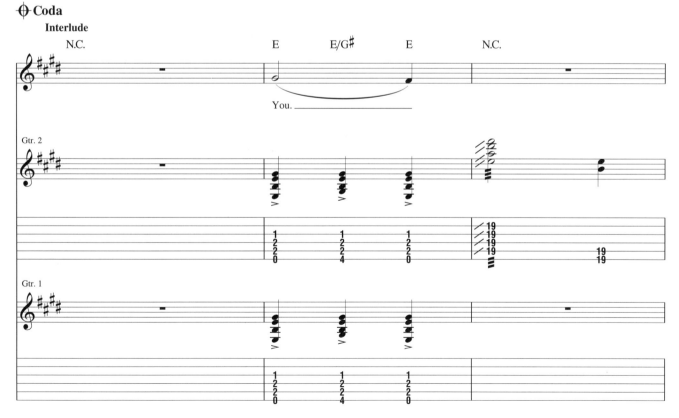

You. _____

Gtr. 2

Gtr. 1

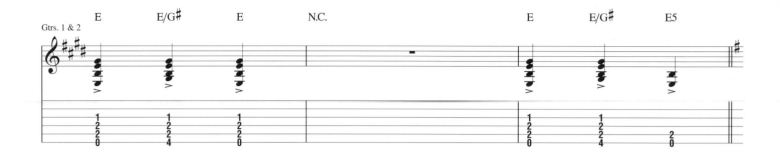

Guitar Solo

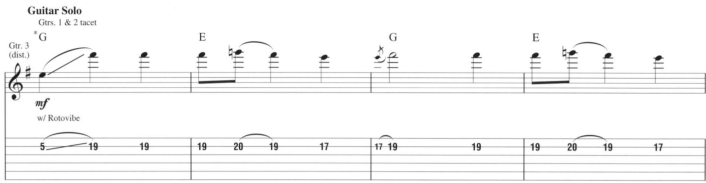

*Chord symbols implied by bass.

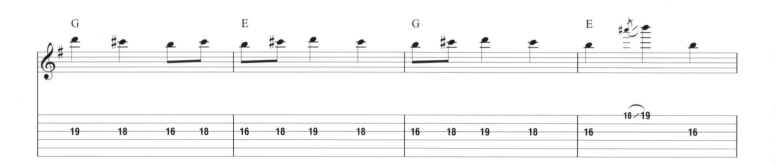

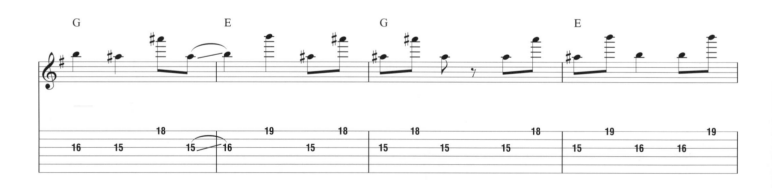

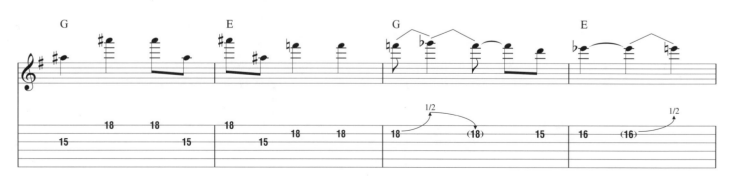

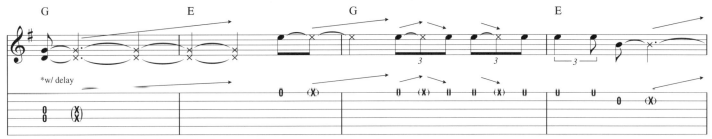

*Delay speed is controlled using foot pedal (toe down = speed increase, toe up = speed decrease).
 Notes tied to X's indicate starting pitch, X's represent delay speed.
 Arrows above X's indicate acceleration/deceleration of delay speed
 (upward arrow = speed increase, downward arrow = speed decrease).

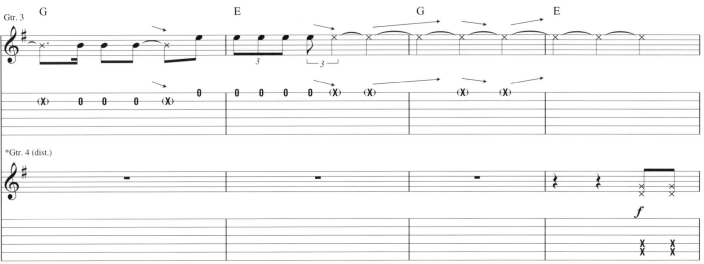

*Doubled throughout

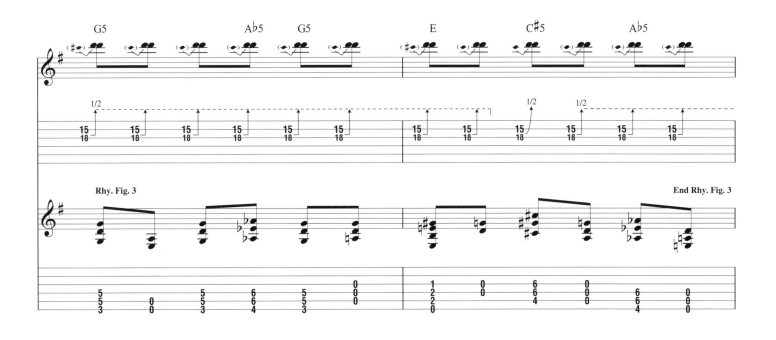

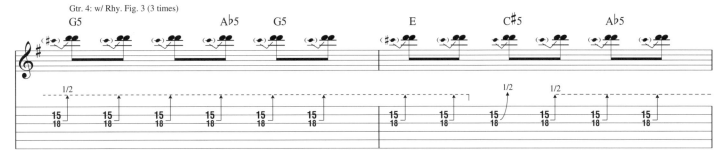

Chorus

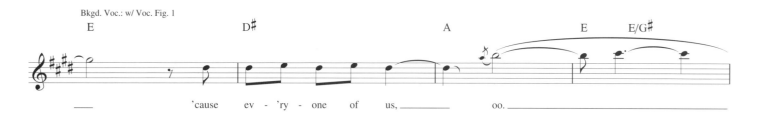

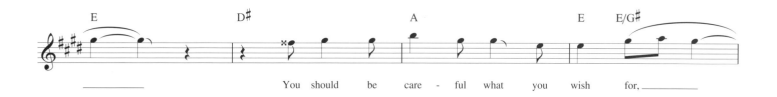

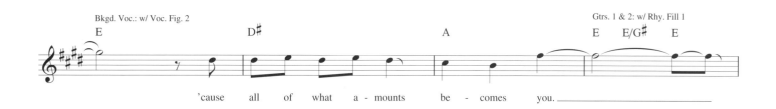

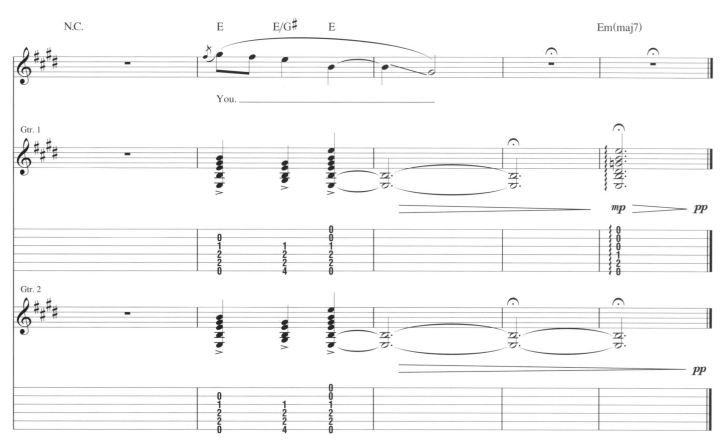

Made for TV Movie

Words and Music by Brandon Boyd, Michael Einziger, Jose Pasillas II, Chris Kilmore and Ben Kenney

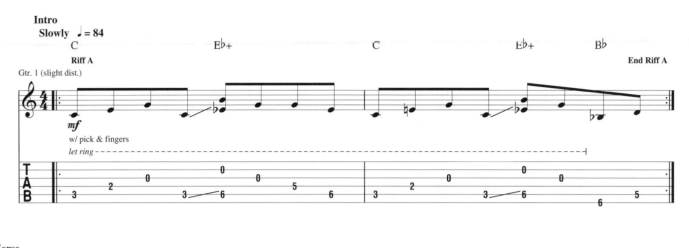

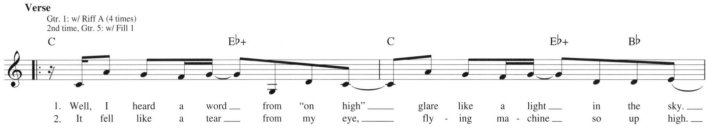

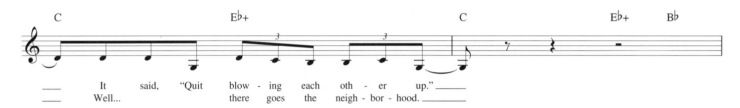

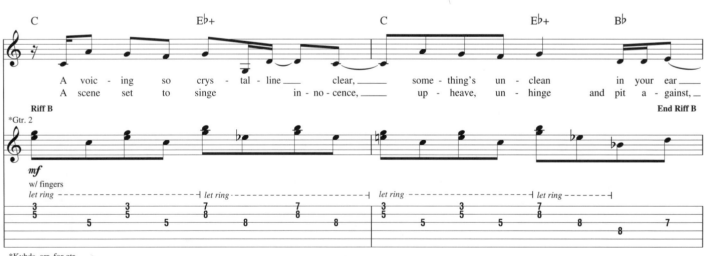

*Kybds. arr. for gtr.

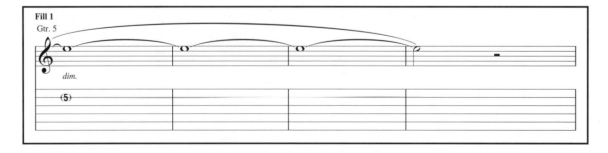

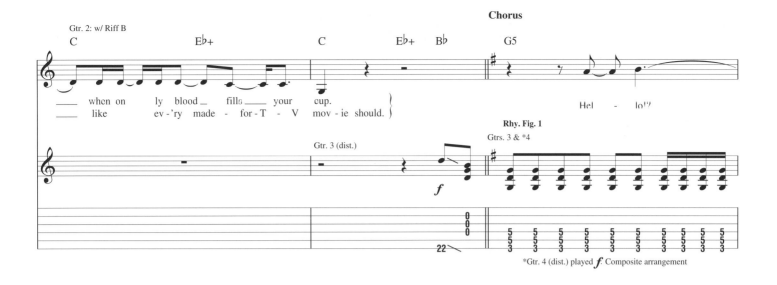

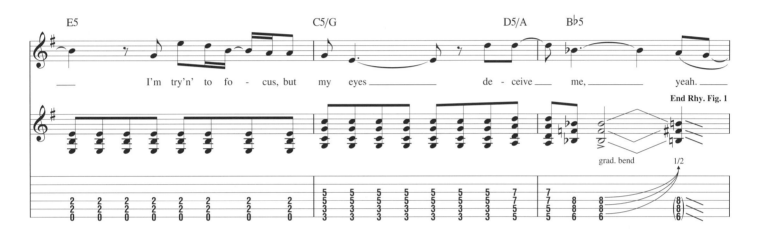

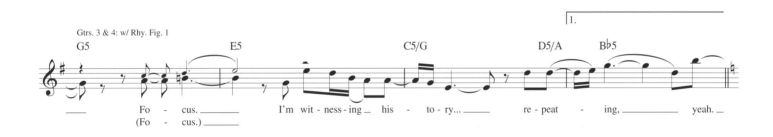

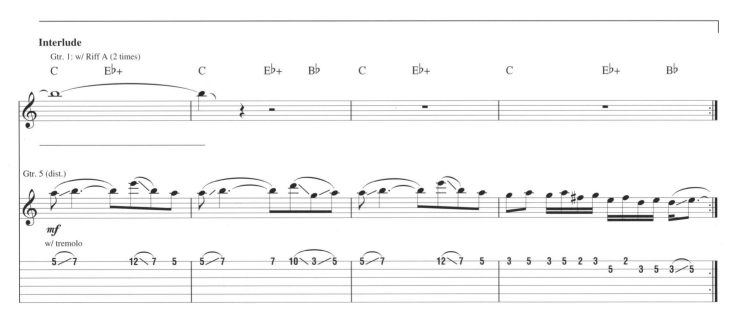

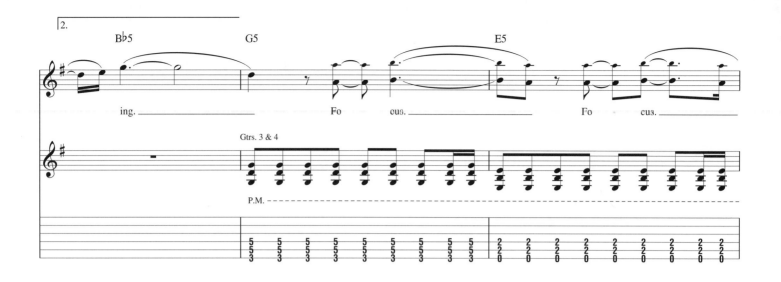

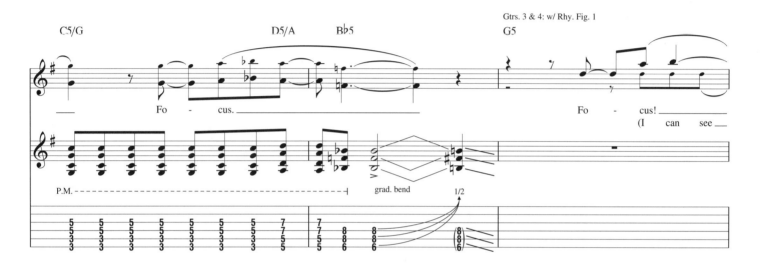

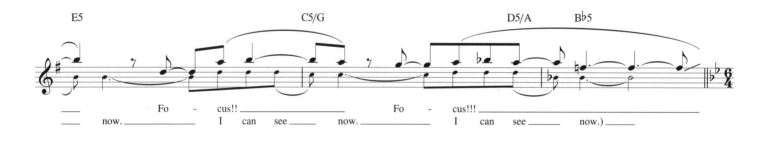

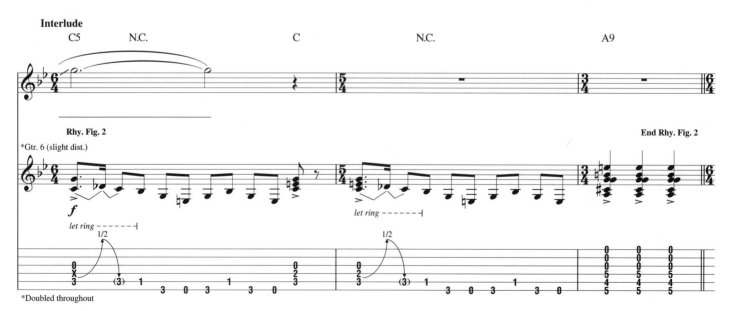

Bridge

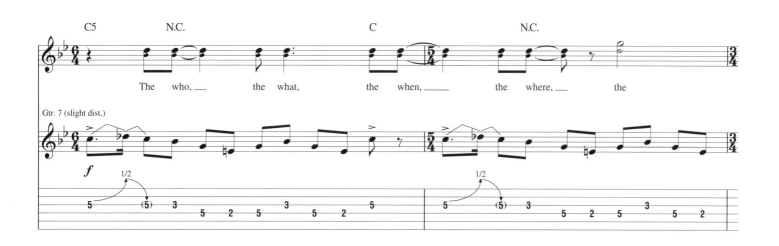

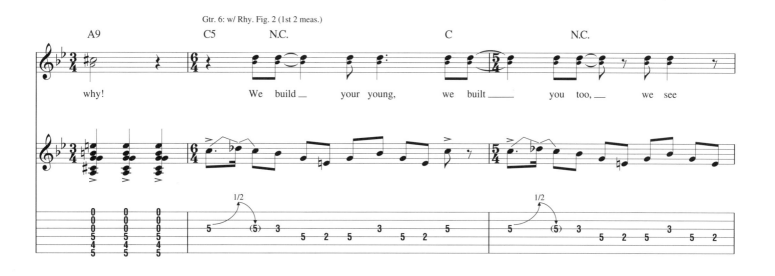

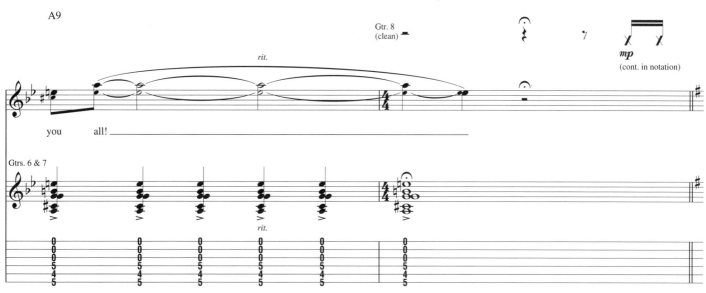

Outro-Chorus
A tempo

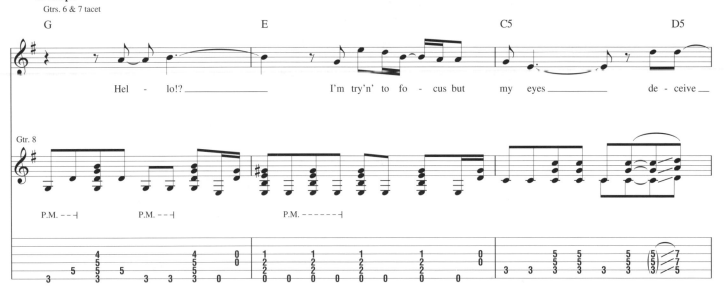

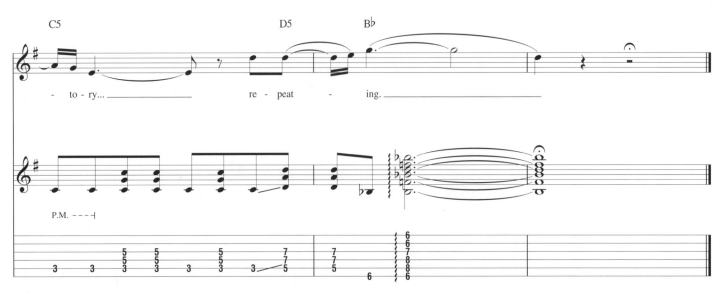

Smile Lines

Words and Music by Brandon Boyd, Michael Einziger, Jose Pasillas II, Chris Kilmore and Ben Kenney

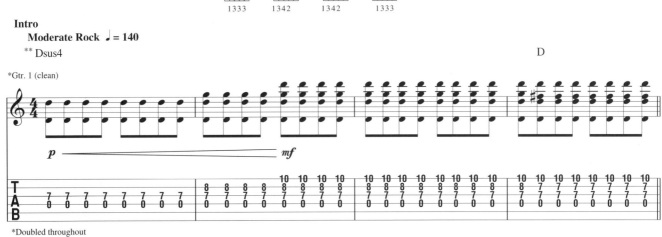

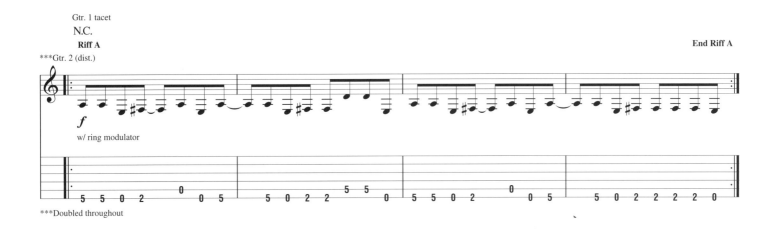

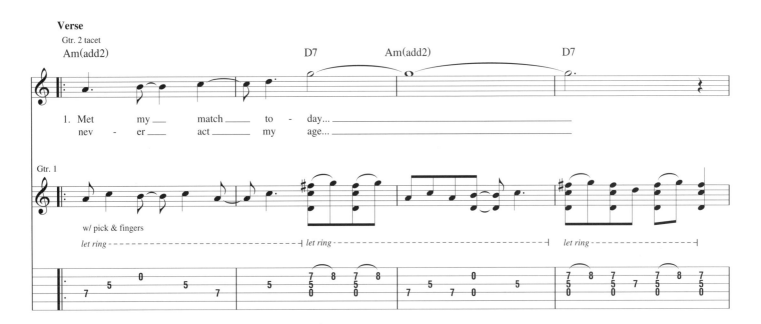

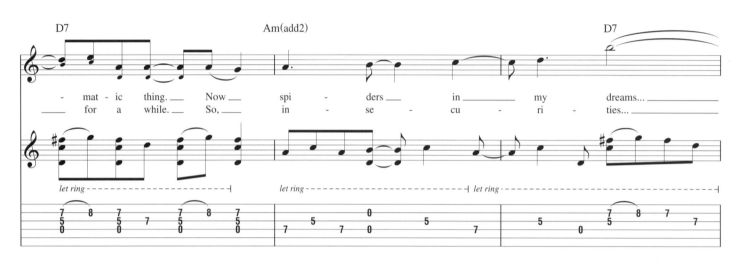

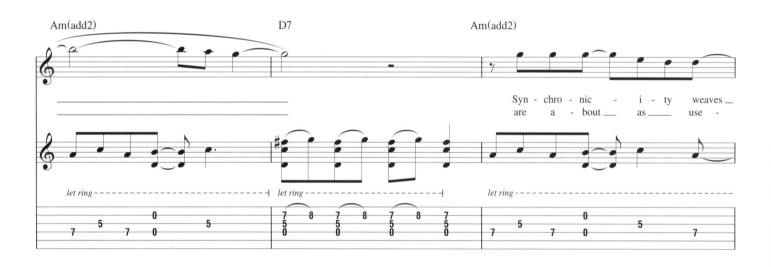

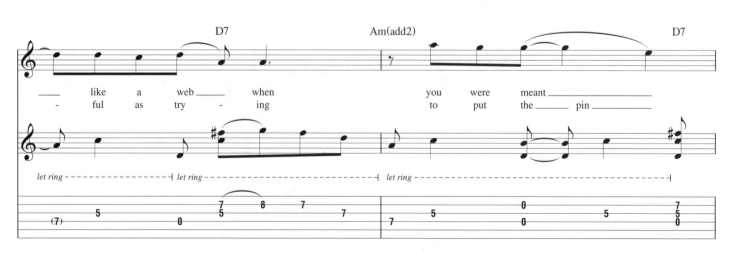

*Composite arrangement

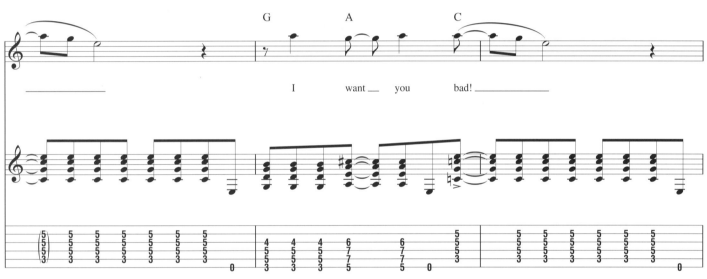

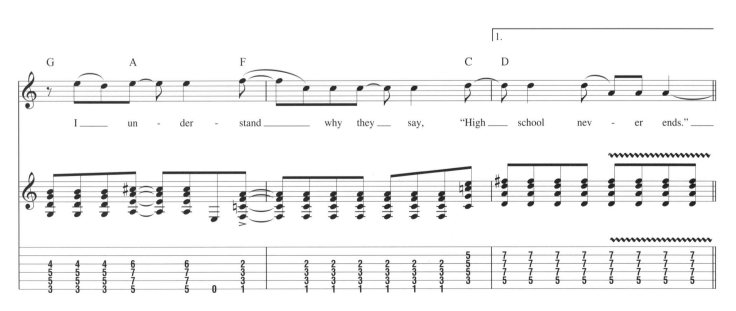

Interlude

Gtrs. 1 & 3 tacet
Gtr. 2: w/ Riff A

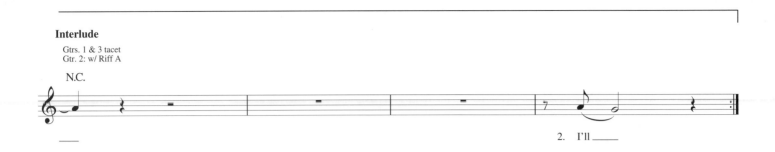

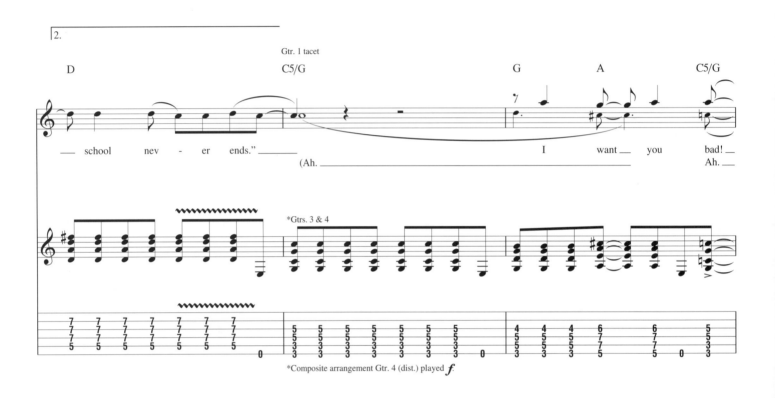

*Composite arrangement Gtr. 4 (dist.) played *f*.

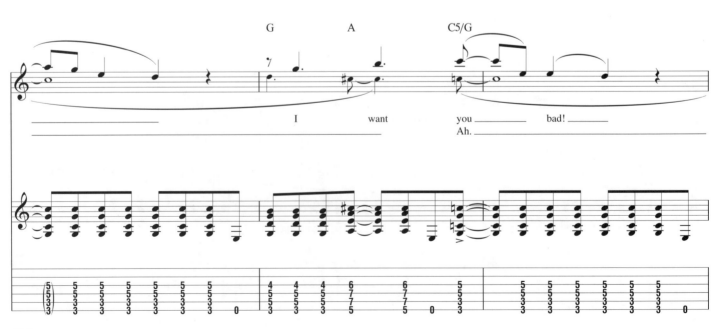

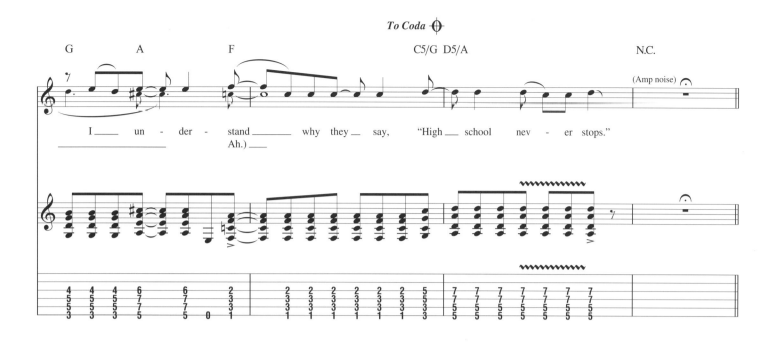

I understand why they say, "High school never stops."
(Ah.)

Interlude

Whoa. Oo, yeah.

Gtrs. 3 & 4: w/ Rhy. Fig. 1

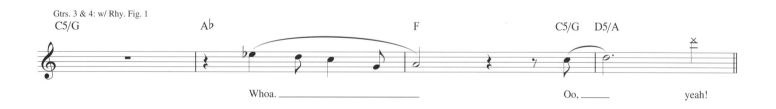

Whoa. Oo, yeah!

Guitar Solo

Gtrs. 3 & 4: w/ Rhy. Fig. 1 (2 times)

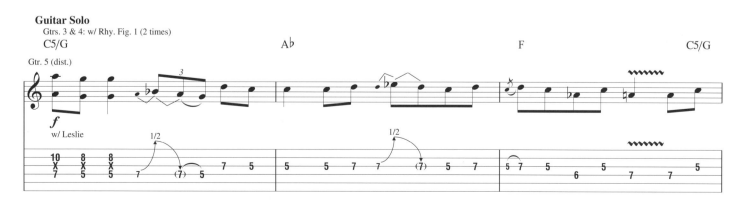

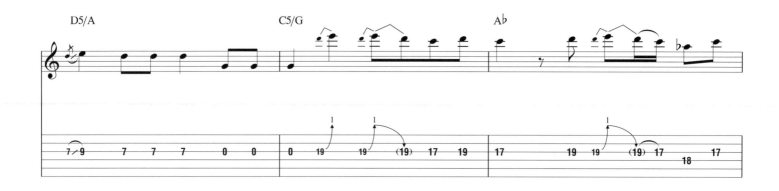

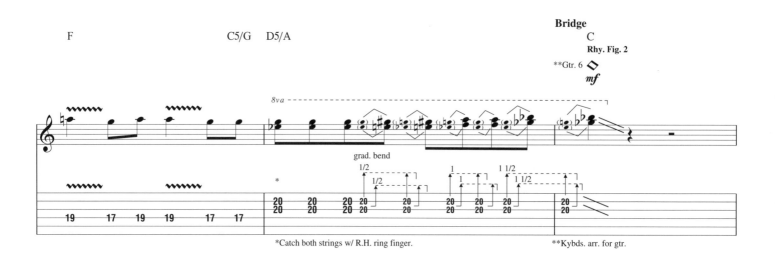

*Catch both strings w/ R.H. ring finger. **Kybds. arr. for gtr.

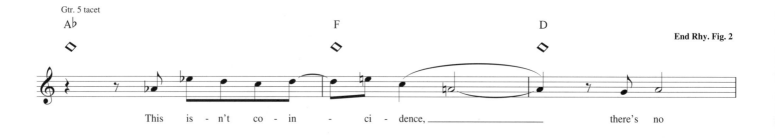

This is - n't co - in - ci - dence,_____ there's no

such thing. ___ This is - n't co - in - ci - dence,_____ no. ___

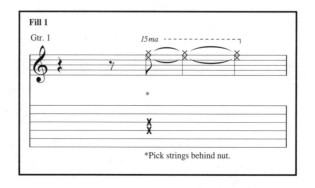

*Pick strings behind nut.

This is - n't co - in - ci - dence, _____ there's no

D.S. al Coda
(take 2nd ending)

such thing. ___ This is - n't, _____ no. _____

⊕ Coda

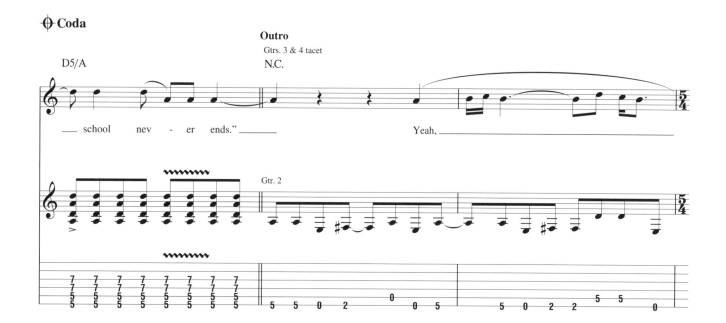

___ school nev - er ends." _____ Yeah,

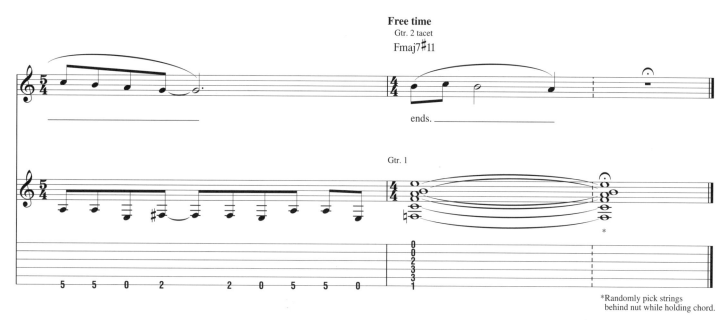

ends. _____

*Randomly pick strings
behind nut while holding chord.

Here in My Room

Words and Music by Brandon Boyd, Michael Einziger, Jose Pasillas II, Chris Kilmore and Ben Kenney

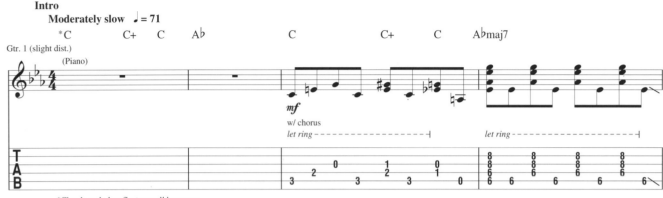

*Chord symbols reflect overall harmony.

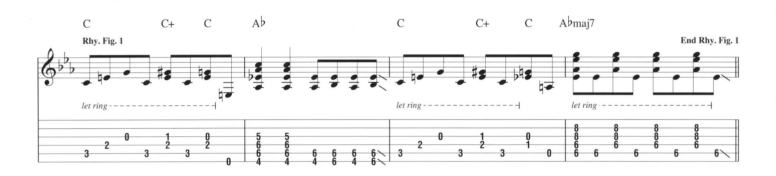

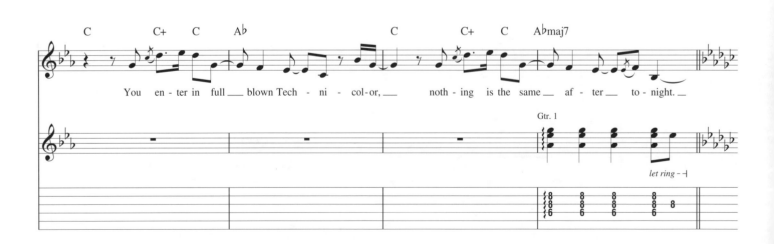

Pre-Chorus

Gtr. 1 tacet

G♭maj13

If the world would fall __ a - part __ in a fic - tion wor - thy wind,

Riff A

Gtr. 2 (slight dist.)

mf

let ring -----------------

Riff A1

Gtr. 3 (slight dist.)

mf

let ring ----------

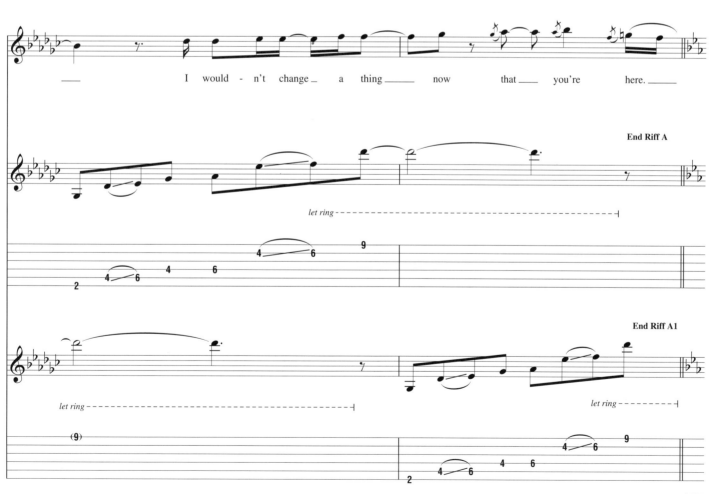

__ I would - n't change __ a thing __ now that __ you're here. __

End Riff A

let ring -----------------

End Riff A1

let ring ----------

let ring ----------

Chorus

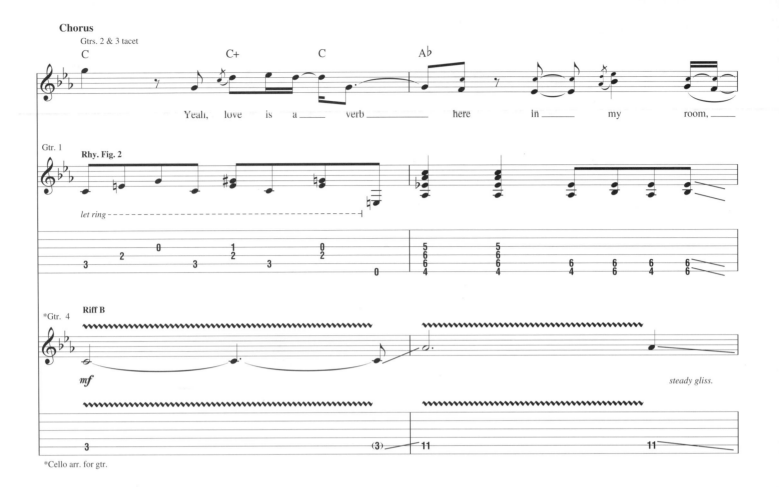

*Cello arr. for gtr.

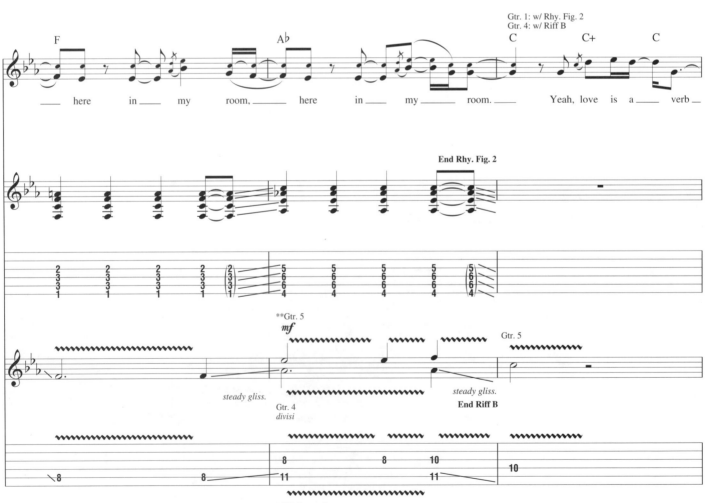

**Violin arr. for gtr.

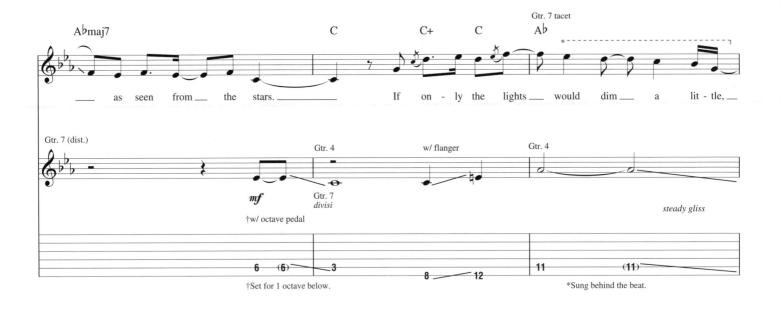

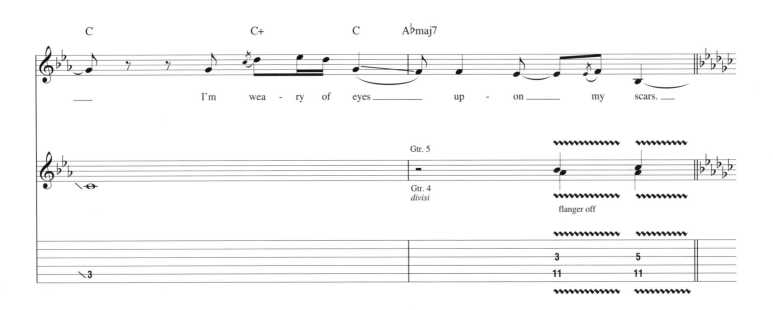

Pre-Chorus

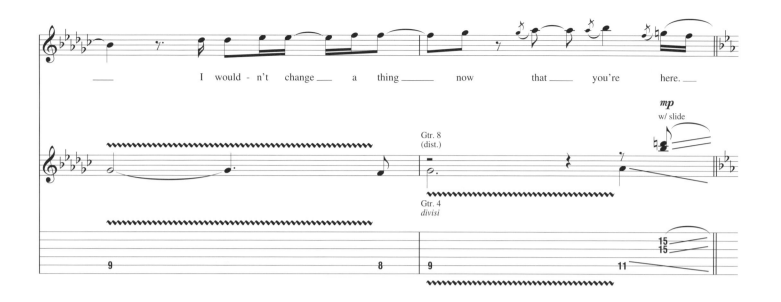

I would-n't change ___ a thing ___ now that ___ you're here. ___

Chorus

Gtr. 1: w/ Rhy. Fig. 2 (2 times)
Gtr. 4: w/ Riff B (2 times)

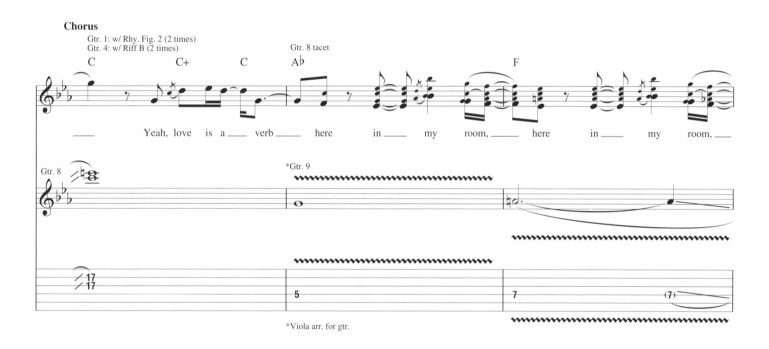

___ Yeah, love is a ___ verb ___ here in ___ my room, ___ here in ___ my room, ___

*Viola arr. for gtr.

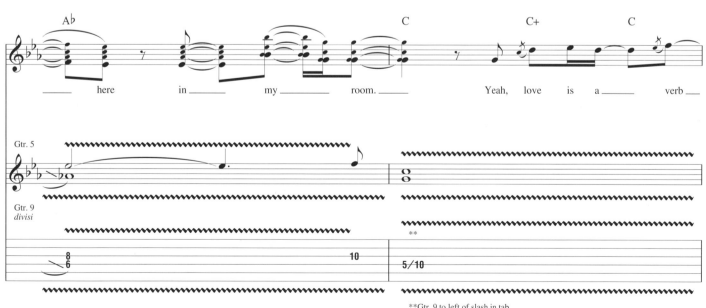

___ here in ___ my ___ room. ___ Yeah, love is a ___ verb ___

**Gtr. 9 to left of slash in tab.

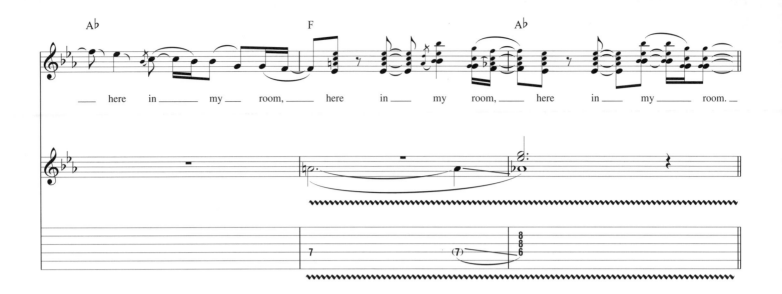

here in ___ my ___ room, ___ here in ___ my ___ room, ___ here in ___ my ___ room. ___

Verse

Gtr. 1: w/ Rhy. Fig. 2 (1 3/4 times)
Gtr. 4: w/ Riff B (1 3/4 times)
Gtrs. 5 & 9 tacet

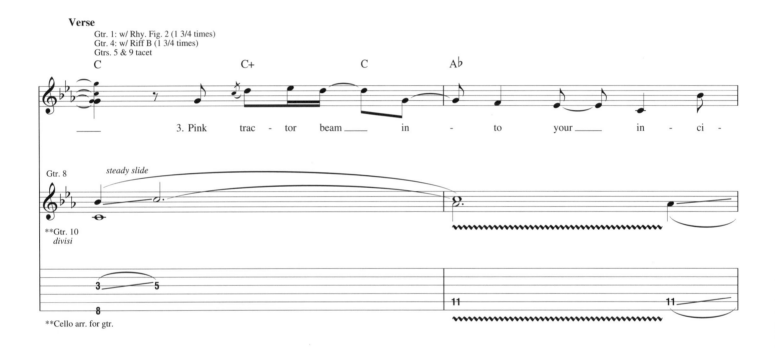

3. Pink trac - tor beam ___ in - to your ___ in - ci -

Gtr. 8
steady slide

**Gtr. 10
divisi

**Cello arr. for gtr.

Gtr. 8 tacet

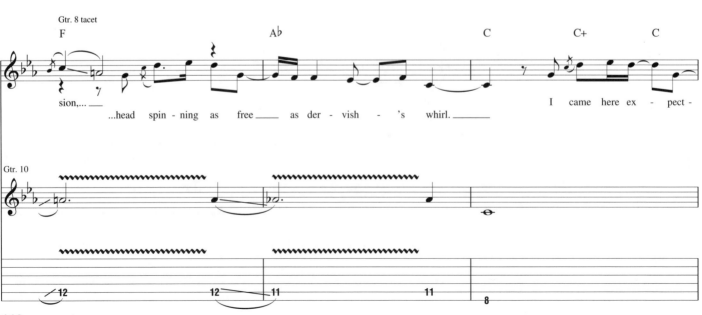

sion,... ...head spin - ning as free ___ as der - vish - 's whirl. ___ I came here ex - pect -

Gtr. 10

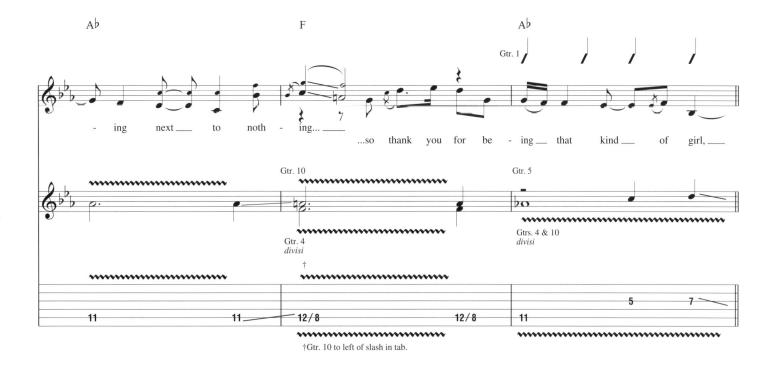

†Gtr. 10 to left of slash in tab.

Outro

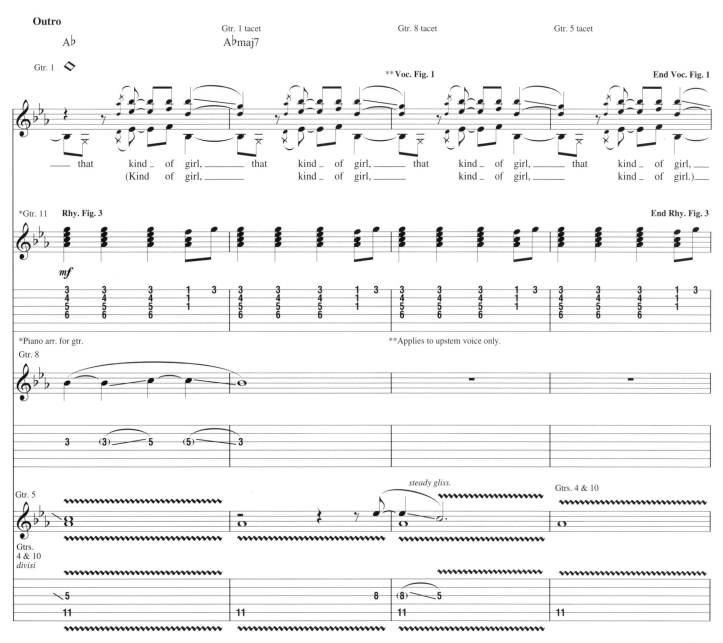

*Piano arr. for gtr.   **Applies to upstem voice only.

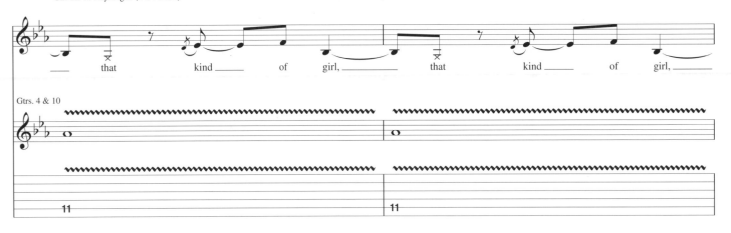

Gtrs. 4 & 10

that   kind ____ of   girl, _____ that   kind ____ of   girl, _____

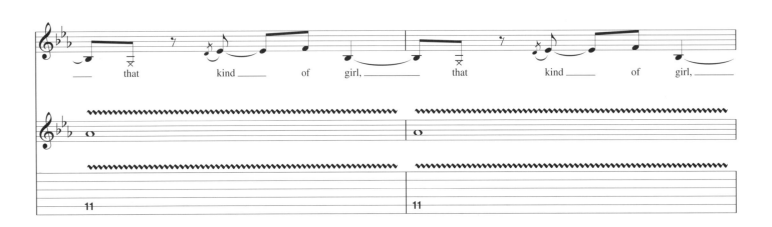

that   kind ____ of   girl, _____ that   kind ____ of   girl, _____

Fade out

rit.

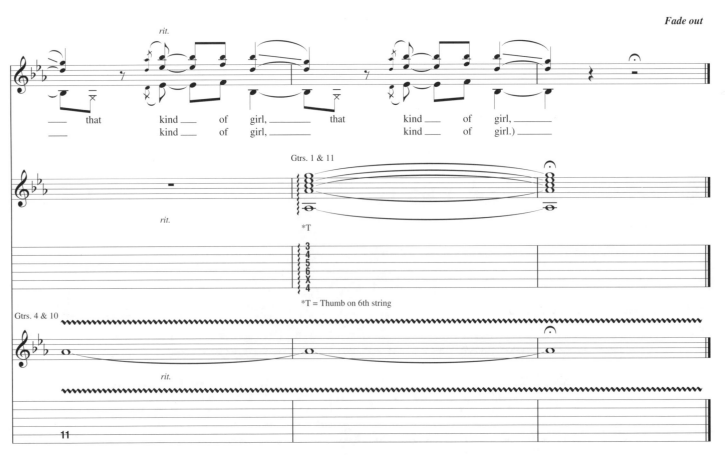

that   kind ___ of   girl, _____ that   kind ___ of   girl, _____
kind ___ of   girl, _____   kind ___ of   girl.)

Gtrs. 1 & 11

rit.

*T

*T = Thumb on 6th string

Gtrs. 4 & 10

rit.

Leech

Words and Music by Brandon Boyd, Michael Einziger, Jose Pasillas II, Chris Kilmore and Ben Kenney

Intro

Fast Rock ♩ = 176

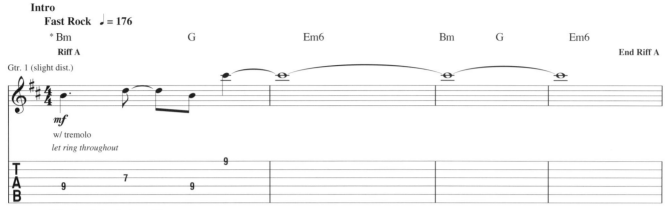

*Chord symbols reflect overall harmony.

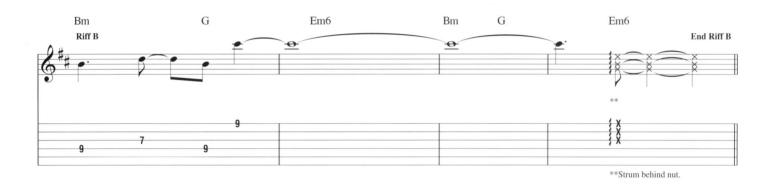

**Strum behind nut.

Verse

1st time, Gtr. 1: w/ Riff A (3 times)
2nd time, Gtr. 1: w/ Riff B
2nd time, Gtr. 2 tacet

1. Uh, does it make you in - die? Does it make you proud,
2. It is - n't fair to men - tion, but it awes the crowd...

2nd time, Gtr. 1: w/ Riff A (2 times)

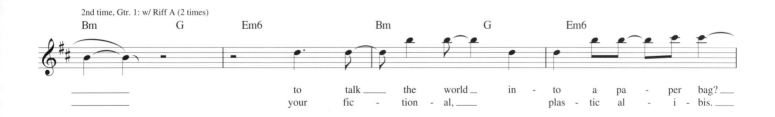

to talk the world in - to a pa - per bag?
your fic - tion - al, plas - tic al - i - bis.

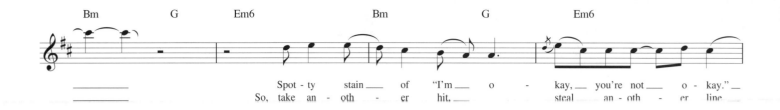

Spot - ty stain ___ of "I'm ___ o - kay, ___ you're not ___ o - kay." ___
So, take an - oth - er hit, ___ steal an - oth - er line.

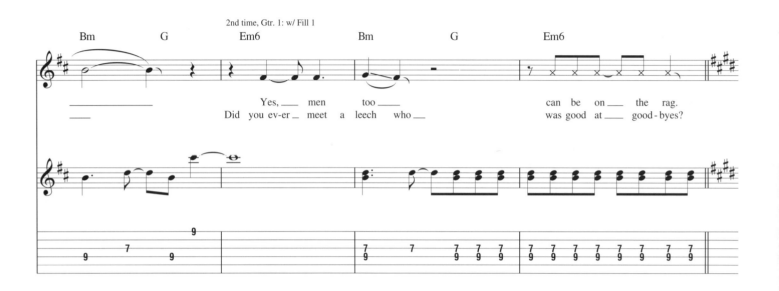

2nd time, Gtr. 1: w/ Fill 1

Yes, ___ men too ___ can be on ___ the rag.
Did you ev-er ___ meet a leech who ___ was good at ___ good - byes?

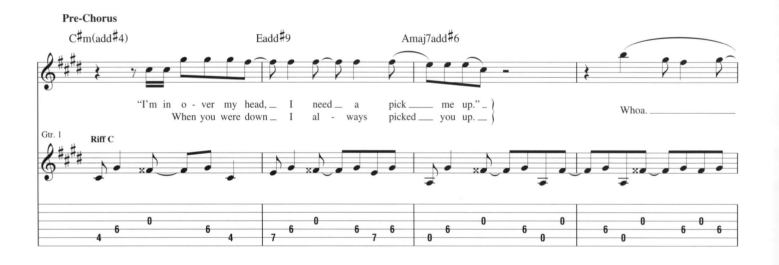

Pre-Chorus

"I'm in o - ver my head, ___ I need ___ a pick ___ me up." ⎱
When you were down ___ I al - ways picked ___ you up. ⎰

Whoa. ___

Gtr. 1

Riff C

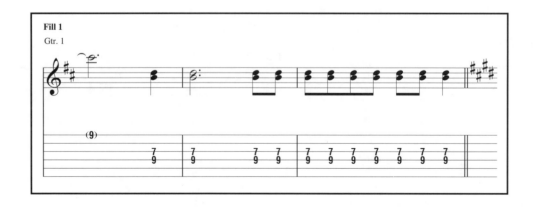

Fill 1

Gtr. 1

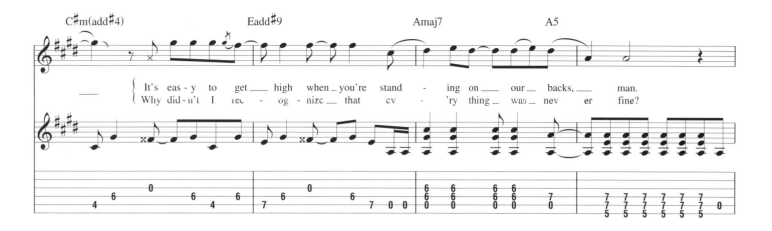

It's eas-y to get ___ high when ___ you're stand ___ ing on ___ our backs, ___ man.
Why did-n't I rec-og-nize that ev-'ry-thing ___ was nev-er fine?

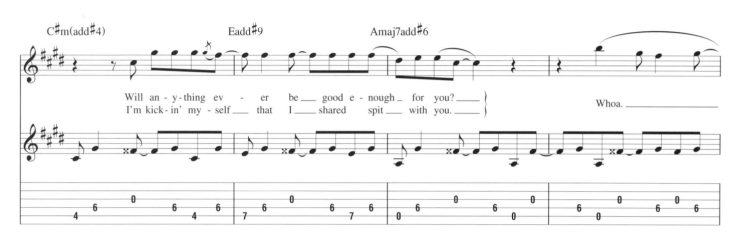

Will an-y-thing ev-er be ___ good e-nough ___ for you? ___
I'm kick-in' my-self ___ that I ___ shared spit with you. ___

Whoa. ___

Stand on your own, ___ hold ___ your wa ___ ter if ___ you can. ___
So, fuck your-self ___ and fuck ___ this bleed ___ ing heart ___ of mine.

*Two gtrs. arr. for one.

The ride's ___ o ___ ver. Did ___ you ___ en-joy your-self?

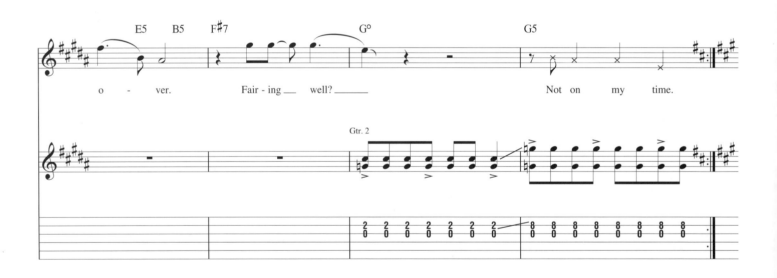

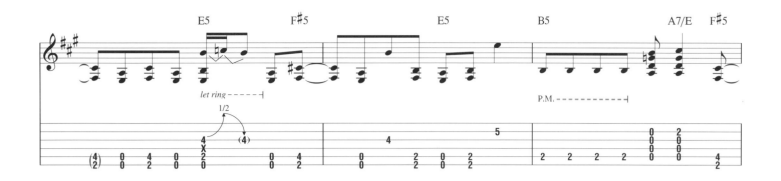

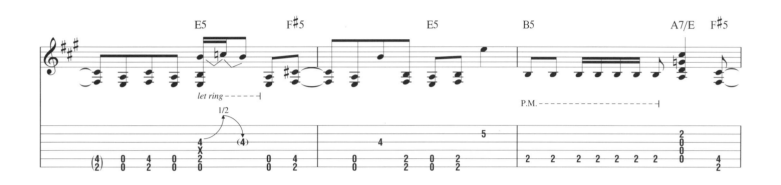

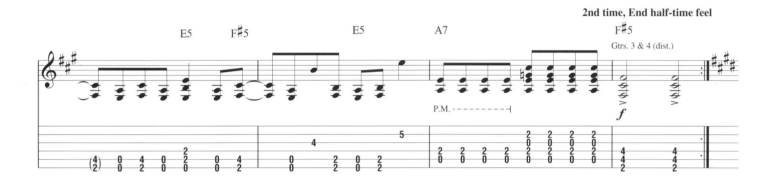

2nd time, End half-time feel

Gtrs. 3 & 4 (dist.)

Pre-Chorus

Gtr. 1: w/ Riff C
Gtrs. 3 & 4 tacet

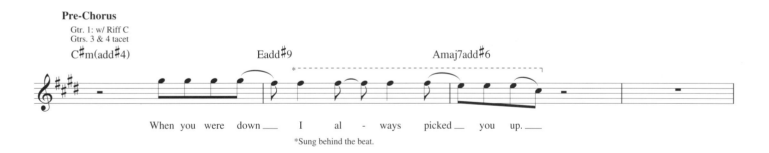

When you were down ___ I al - ways picked ___ you up. ___

*Sung behind the beat.

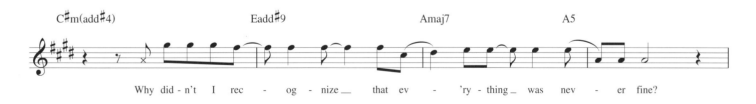

Why did - n't I rec - og - nize ___ that ev - 'ry - thing ___ was nev - er fine?

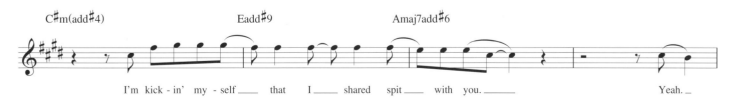

I'm kick - in' my - self ___ that I ___ shared spit with you. ___   Yeah. ___

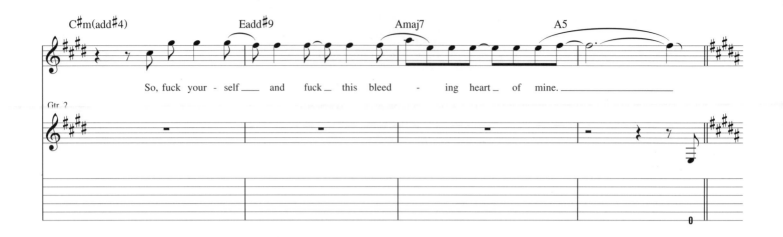

So, fuck your - self ___ and fuck ___ this bleed - ing heart ___ of mine. ___

Chorus

Gtr. 2: w/ Rhy. Fig. 1

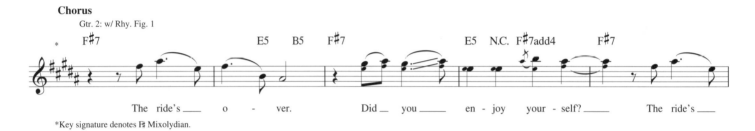

The ride's ___ o - ver. Did ___ you ___ en - joy your - self? ___ The ride's ___

*Key signature denotes F♮ Mixolydian.

Gtr. 2: w/ Rhy. Fig. 1 (1st 2 meas.) (4 times)

o - ver. Fair - ing ___ well? The ride's ___ o - ver.

Did ___ you ___ en - joy your - self? ___ The ride's ___ o - ver.

Outro-Chorus

Gtr. 2: w/ Rhy. Fig. 1 (1st 2 meas.) (till fade)

Fair - ing ___ well? ___ The ride's ___ o - ver. The ride's ___

o - ver. The ride's ___ o - ver. The ride's ___ o - ver.

Play 4 times and fade

The ride's ___ o - ver. The ride's ___ o - ver.